FOUNT CHRISTIAN THINKERS

Thomas More

ANNE MURPHY

Anne Murphy is a member of the Society of
the Holy Child. She studied History and
Theology at the University of London, and
obtained her doctorate from the Gregorian
University, Rome. She currently lectures
in Reformation Studies and Systematic
Theology at Heythrop College, University of
London. Her previous work includes *The
Theology of the Cross in the Prison Writings of
Saint Thomas More*.

The series editor, Dr Peter Vardy, is lecturer
in the Philosophy of Religion at Heythrop
College. He is a former Chair of the
Theology Faculty Board of the University of
London. His previous books published by
Fount Paperbacks are *The Puzzle of God*, *The
Puzzle of Evil*, *The Puzzle of Ethics* and *The
Puzzle of the Gospels*, and he is currently
planning a fifth in the bestselling series.

THE FOUNT CHRISTIAN THINKERS SERIES

AUGUSTINE Richard Price
'... admirably clear, concise, and, though sometimes critical, written with great sympathy and understanding of Augustine's problems, and of the historical context within which he was labouring.' MICHAEL WALSH

FRANCIS & BONAVENTURE Paul Rout
'This book meets a real need ... a painless way into Bonaventure's life and thinking, both as a philosopher, a man of prayer and as a great Franciscan.' SISTER FRANCES TERESA, OSC, THE COMMUNITY OF THE POOR CLARES, ARUNDEL

JOHN OF THE CROSS Wilfrid McGreal
'We are greatly indebted to Fr Wilfrid McGreal for bringing alive in such an accessible way the mysticism and mystery of St John of the Cross.' GEORGE CAREY, ARCHBISHOP OF CANTERBURY

THOMAS MORE Anne Murphy
'This superb piece of scholarship sheds new light on the enduring importance of the unity between Thomas More's life and thought. Anne Murphy shows how this large-hearted Christian was a great European and an outstanding example of personal and public integrity.' GERALD O'COLLINS, GREGORIAN UNIVERSITY, ROME

KIERKEGAARD Peter Vardy
'This is a fascinating introduction to Kierkegaard's prophetic insights into the nature of Christian faith, insights which we desperately need to ponder today.' GERARD HUGHES, AUTHOR OF GOD OF SURPRISES

SIMONE WEIL Stephen Plant
'Stephen Plant portrays the immense strength and the touching vulnerability of Simone Weil, the complex nature of her convictions, and the startling and continuing relevance of her views today.' DONALD ENGLISH, CHAIRMAN OF THE WORLD METHODIST COUNCIL

FORTHCOMING
LUTHER Hans-Peter Grosshans
KARL RAHNER Karen Kilby
EVELYN UNDERHILL Ann Loades

FOUNT CHRISTIAN THINKERS

THOMAS MORE

Anne Murphy

SERIES EDITOR: PETER VARDY

Fount

An Imprint of HarperCollins*Publishers*

For
Elisabeth Jupp and Jared Wicks

Fount Paperbacks is an Imprint of
HarperCollins*Religious*
Part of HarperCollins*Publishers*
77–85 Fulham Palace Road, London W6 8JB

First published in Great Britain
in 1996 by Fount Paperbacks

1 3 5 7 9 10 8 6 4 2

A catalogue record for this book is
available from the British Library

ISBN 0 00 627914 7

Printed and bound in Great Britain by
Caledonian International Book Manufacturing Ltd, Glasgow

Contents

Abbreviations

The following abbreviations are used in references given in the text:

CW   The Yale Edition of the *Complete Works of St Thomas More*

CW5   *Responsio ad Lutherum*, ed. J. M. Headley

CW6   *A Dialogue Concerning Heresies*, eds. T. Lawler, G. Marc'hadour, R. Marius

CW8   *The Confutation of Tyndale's Answer*, eds. L. A. Schuster, R. Marius, J. P. Luscardi, R. J. Schoeck

CW12   *A Dialogue of Comfort against Tribulation*, eds. L. L. Martz and F. Manley

CW13   *Treatise on the Passion*, ed. G. E. Haupt

CW15   *In Defence of Humanism*, ed. D. Kinney

DC   *A Dialogue of Comfort against Tribulation*, ed. F. Manley

EA   *Essential Articles for the Study of Thomas More*, ed. R. S. Sylvester and G. Marc'hadour

Gogan   B. Gogan, *The Common Corps of Christendom*

Harpsfield   Nicholas Harpsfield, *Life of More*

HR3   *The History of King Richard III & Selections from Poems*, ed. R. S. Sylvester

Kenny   A. Kenny, *Thomas More*

LW   *Luther's Works*, eds. J. Pelikan, H. T. Lehmann

Martz   L. Martz, *Thomas More: The Search for the Inner Man*

Moreana   *Moreana, Bulletin of Amici Thomae Mori*, Angers 1963–

Roper   W. Roper, *The Life of Sir Thomas More*

Rogers   *The Correspondence of Sir Thomas More*, ed. E. F. Rogers

SL   *St Thomas More: Selected Letters*, ed. E. F. Rogers

TW   *Thomas More: The Tower Works*, ed. G. E. Haupt

U   *Utopia*, ed. G. M. Logan & R. M. Adams

Full bibliographical details of these and other works are given in Suggested Further Reading.

Date Chart

Early Life

1477/8	Born in parish of St Lawrence Jewry, city of London
c.1492	Oxford University
1496	Admitted to Lincoln's Inn, London
1499	First meeting with Erasmus on his visit to England
1505	Married Jane Colt: four children: Margaret, Elizabeth, Cecily, John
1509	Accession of Henry VIII
	Erasmus writes *In Praise of Folly* in More's house
1510	Under-Sheriff of London. Elected to Parliament
1511	Wife died; remarried to Alice Middleton
1513–18	*History of King Richard III* (English and Latin versions)

Public Life

1515	Flanders mission. Book 2 of *Utopia* written in Antwerp
1516	*Utopia* completed and published
1517	Became a member of the King's Council
1523	Elected Speaker of the House of Commons
1525	Appointed Chancellor to the Duchy of Lancaster
1527	Proceedings to annul Henry VIII's marriage to Catherine of Aragon
1528	Licensed to read, retain and confute Protestant writings
1529	Succeeded Wolsey as Lord Chancellor of England
1532	Resigned as Chancellor

1533   Henry married Anne Boleyn
1534   Imprisoned for refusing oath to Act of Succession

Polemical Writings

1521   Luther condemned at the Diet of Worms
1523   More's *Responsio ad Lutherum*
1526   *Letter to Bugenhagen*
       Tyndale's translation of New Testament reaches
       England
1529   *A Dialogue Concerning Heresies* (revised 1531)
       Supplication of Souls
1532/3 *Confutation of Tyndale's Answer* (about 500,000 words)
       Letter to John Frith
1533   *Apology*
       Debellation of Salem & Bizance
       An Answer to a Poisoned Book

Prison Writings

1534   *A Treatise on the Passion.* Begun, possibly finished before
       prison
       A Dialogue of Comfort Against Tribulation
1535   *De Tristitia Christi* (original manuscript found in 1963,
       Valentia)
       Letters from prison, prayers, annotations in Psalter
       Trial proceedings and execution July 1535

Posthumous Reputation

1935   Canonization of John Fisher and Thomas More
1963–1996   Yale edition of *Complete Works of St Thomas More*

Introduction

The Controversial Thomas More

I cannot tell whether I would call him a foolish wise man or a
wise foolish man.   (EDWARD HALL, CHRONICLER)

Thomas More is remembered most often as the author of *Utopia*, a
classic of political thought, and as a former Lord Chancellor of
England, executed for treason against Henry VIII because he
refused to take an oath against his conscience. In time the manner of his dying, with courage and understated humour, won him
the admiration of those who did not share his religious convictions. Jonathan Swift regarded him as 'a person of greatest virtue
this kingdom has ever produced'; Macaulay, who could not
understand the beliefs for which More died, regarded him as 'one
of the choice specimens of human wisdom and virtue'. Most
would agree that More is someone whose life and thought will
always reward greater study, because of their continued relevance to our own human choices and situations.

Contemporary scholarship, however, has revealed that Thomas
More was a far more controversial figure in his life, death and
posthumous reputation than we might have been led to believe.
When he was beheaded in the Tower of London on 6 July 1535,
few, if any, of his family and friends understood why his 'scruple of
conscience' should have brought about his death. His friend, the
Dutch scholar Desiderius Erasmus, commented: 'Would that he
had never become involved in such a dangerous matter, and had
left theological business to theologians.' His daughter, Margaret,

herself took the oath he had refused. His wife, Alice, put the family point of view most vigorously: 'Master More, I would marvel that you, that have been always ... taken for so wise a man, will now so play the fool.' Most of More's contemporaries agreed with Alice's common-sense view.

It was only slowly and with hindsight that More's family and close friends came to understand the religious and political consequences of Henry VIII's quarrel with the Pope, his claim to Royal Supremacy over the Church in England, and so the reasons for More's resistance. As they lovingly preserved his relics and collated his writings, they began to interpret More as a Catholic martyr who died for the orthodoxy of his faith. To make this saintly More better known and loved, they published More's English works (1557) and his Latin works (1565). The saintly image of More influenced William Roper's first family 'memoir' of his father-in-law, and the four subsequent 'biographies' written between 1557 and 1631. As English Catholics were reduced to a persecuted minority at home, or were forced into exile, they came to see More through the lens of their own suffering, and kept alive the memory of More as martyr and saint. However they neglected or played down his reputation as humanist writer and friend of Erasmus.

In the earlier part of their lives (c.1500–20), More, Erasmus and their circle of friends had aimed at the reform of the Church in 'head and members'. This involved quite strong criticism of many aspects of Christian life and practice. But from 1517 onwards, the coming of Martin Luther and the Protestant Reformations meant that the language of reform became suspect in Catholic circles. More's orthodox reputation would not be helped by mentioning his closeness to Erasmus, whose writings were put on the Roman list of books forbidden to be read by Catholics (1558). Some of More's own earlier views on the papacy and the reform of Christendom were either toned down or edited out of his writings. It was the Basle edition of More's works

(1563) that presented him again as humanist writer and reformer. Contemporary scholarship has paid most attention to this tradition of More.

In his highly successful play *A Man for All Seasons* (1960), Robert Bolt presents More as a man with 'an adamantine sense of his own self'. What fascinated him was the drama of an individual conscience holding out against the power of a tyrant. In the present century we are interested in human rights and the freedom of the individual conscience, in ways that would have been very unfamiliar to More. Bolt admired More as a 'hero of selfhood'. But More saw the human self as 'in the hands of God', not as independent or free-standing. This raises the problem of how far we are justified in interpreting More in the light of our own interests and concerns. His context may be like, but does not replicate, our own.

With the exception of *Utopia*, which has received much attention, More's contribution as a Christian thinker and writer has been neglected until relatively recently. In 1963 Yale University initiated a project to provide a critical, scholarly edition of the *Complete Works of St Thomas More*. This is just nearing completion (1996) and has enabled a much fuller appreciation of all More's writings – humanist, polemical and devotional. We can evaluate him as a humanist who argued for moral, social and religious reform, and as a lay theologian whose views on the nature of the Church were rich and creative. But we may be less appreciative of the combative and adversarial style he used when he wrote in defence of his faith. The devotional and religious intensity of his prison writings belong to the finest of that genre within the whole Christian tradition.

In the light of this 'new' material, a revisionist school of historians has set out to uncover the 'real Thomas More', sanctified and exalted by a series of admiring and uncritical biographers, from Roper (1557) to Chambers (1935). They challenged the traditional view of More as a humane, wise, heroic 'man for all seasons'. In his biography (1985) Richard Marius wanted to discover the 'man of flesh and blood able to take his place in his real world, and ours.' An extreme revisionist thesis affirms that the 'real Thomas More' was a singularly unattractive character, ambitious, intolerant, reactionary and guilt-ridden, a 'man who tried to salvage his failing reputation by a final act of stage-managed heroism'.

While this exercise was long overdue, it is itself deserving of criticism. 'The all too human More of the revisionists constitutes as great a travesty as the all too saintly More of the hagiographers' (B. Bradshaw, 'The Controversial Sir Thomas More', *Journal of Ecclesiastical History*, 1985, 536). Recent studies have moved beyond the somewhat sterile arguments surrounding the 'real Thomas More', and recognize that thirty years of research have cleaned away the overlay on his traditionally gilded portrait. The process has revealed details obscured or unknown to previous generations. The restored portrait is the same portrait, 'warts and all', not an entirely new painting. The revisionist challenge has, if anything, enhanced our appreciation of the creativity and humanity of an outstanding Christian thinker, whose fate it was to have to test his ideals and thought in the public arena of practical politics and religion.

Early Life and Marriage
1478–1515

More is a man of an angel's wit and singular learning; I know not his fellow. For where is the man of that gentleness, lowliness and affability? As time requireth a man of marvellous mirth and pastimes; and sometimes of as sad gravity; a man for all seasons.
(RICHARD WHITTINTON, 1520)

Thomas More was born in London in 1477 or 1478, in the last years of the reign of Edward IV (1461–1483), and he lived there for most of his life. Its sights and sounds and common talk were to shape the direction of his thought, which was urban and community-centred, and salted with earthy common sense. Both his parents came from the upwardly mobile London merchant class, which was ambitious to acquire land and status from its newly acquired wealth. His father, John, became a judge, and chose the legal profession for his son, living until 1530, proud to see Thomas as Lord Chancellor of England. He appears in family portraits and was given marked respect and honour by More. We hear very little about More's mother, Agnes, who died sometime before 1507.

More's education began in St Antony's, Threadneedle Street, a leading London school. Then he was sent to serve as a page at Lambeth Palace, the household of John Morton, Archbishop of Canterbury. This was a training in court life – waiting at table, listening to the conversations of the great and powerful, taking part in amateur dramatics and court entertainment. It gave More a lifelong sense of familiarity and ease in such circles. Morton's patronage enabled him to spend about two years at Oxford University, until his father recalled him to legal studies in London, first at New Inn and then at Lincoln's Inn. He became familiar not only with the principles of English common law but with the 'putting of cases', and the weighing of both sides of an argument. He qualified for the bar in about 1501, and was soon appointed as reader in Furnival's Inn, instructing young students.

Between 1501 and 1505 More 'lived without vow' at the London Charterhouse, home of the Carthusian monks. It was not unusual for young graduates to be associated with this monastery while continuing with their professional lives. Charterhouse was known for its strict observance, religious orthodoxy, and practical piety, and it had a lasting effect on More's spirituality. A time of withdrawal for prayer and reflection was built into his daily and weekly schedule. It is probable that for a time he was attracted to the monastic way of life, but finally opted for marriage and a life of public service.

More, therefore, had four distinct strands to his formal education: court life at Lambeth, Oxford University, legal studies, and a period sharing monastic life and prayer. To this he now added a fifth area of interest, which came to inform and colour his whole outlook. From 1499 onwards he joined a number of friends who were critical of the somewhat sterile and unimaginative educational methods current in schools and universities. Under the influence of John Colet, Dean of St Paul's Cathedral, and a generation of scholars who had been educated in Italy, More and his circle began to share the views of a wider, more diffuse, European movement which later generations labelled **Christian Humanism**. (This is explained more fully in Chapter 2.) They became convinced that any serious renewal of religion and society must begin with a renewal in education, and a retrieval of classical and Christian sources. When the Dutch humanist scholar Desiderius Erasmus visited England in 1499, he forged a lasting friendship with More, and provided a strong link with continental humanism.

More and his friends set about perfecting their Latin and learning Greek. They read the pagan and Christian classics not only for content, but also for form and style. They wanted to be 'men of letters', able to communicate through a well-turned phrase, a good public speech, or a well-constructed letter. Humanists aimed to influence the language or discourse of school, university, pulpit and court – the communications media of the day. They admired the old classical writing styles, especially that of Cicero. So since style was 'the dress of thoughts', More began his humanist career by practising the art of writing and speaking well, in English, Latin and Greek. He translated poems and epigrams, wrote his own poetry, translated the life of Pico della Mirandola (a leading figure of the Italian Renaissance), and wrote the *History of King Richard III*. He also began to read the classics of early Christian theology, especially Jerome, Ambrose and Augustine. This explains why More, a layman, gave a series of lectures on Augustine's *City of God* in a London church *c.*1501.

But More's humanistic studies and writings were only one part of an increasingly busy professional life. He was elected to Parliament, and became Under-Sheriff in the City of London in 1510. As such he was a permanent adviser to the Sheriffs, and sat as judge in the Sheriffs' court at the Guildhall.

In 1505 More married Jane (or Joan) Colt and had four children by her: Margaret, Elizabeth, Cecily and John. They made their home in the Old Barge, Bucklersbury, and it was here that Erasmus wrote *In Praise of Folly* (1509) while More's guest, and where More's *Utopia* was completed (1516). Within a month of Jane's death in 1511, More married Lady Alice Middleton, a widow with one daughter, and known to Jane's family circle. Henry VIII's secretary, Andrea Ammonio, called Alice a 'beak-nosed harpy' and she has had a bad press ever since. The standard view has been that More chose a mere step-mother/housekeeper for his children, and an additional hairshirt for himself. But Lady Alice turns out to have been considerably younger than was thought, wealthy, attractive and fashion-conscious. She was a kinswoman of Henry VIII through the marriage of her cousin, Mary Bohun, into the Tudor family. It would seem that More made an exceptionally advantageous second marriage, which undoubtedly furthered his career, and may have been a spur to his political ambitions.

Whereas Jane had been somewhat in awe of her clever husband, Alice was made of sterner stuff and gave him as good as she got. More certainly enjoyed her company and her repartee, and she often made him laugh – even when he was in prison. She tried to smarten up his appearance and to humanize the rigorous order of the household. But she was also very ambitious for her husband and may have put pressure on him to enter public life. More's epitaph, written (c.1532) for his tomb in Chelsea, makes a succinct statement: 'The one so lived with me, and the other so liveth, that it is doubtful whether this or the other were dearer unto me... O how well could we three have lived joined together in matrimony, if fortune and religion would have suffered it. So death shall give us that thing which life could not.'

Together More and Alice supervised the studies of the children, at least until 1516, when outside tutors were hired. More loved his garden, his aviary and his small menagerie, and he encouraged his children to take an interest in plants and animals. When they were older he also encouraged them to undertake some form of work for the less fortunate. For example, Margaret Giggs, his adopted daughter, visited prisoners in Newgate prison. More himself had a special understanding of, and sympathy for, the mentally handicapped and those with suicidal tendencies.

A Family Portrait

In about 1525 the family moved from their city home to a larger house in Chelsea. Hans Holbein the Younger was welcomed into the house for a time between 1526 and 1528, and painted the famous group portrait of Thomas More at the centre of his family. (Sadly, the original is lost, though the preliminary sketch survives in Basle.) Renaissance portraits are not as innocent as we might once have thought. Such paintings were commissioned and bought to be displayed as indicators of family wealth, position and importance. The Holbein family painting shows how More wished to be remembered by posterity. Every detail included has its special significance.

Erasmus was to describe the household in Chelsea as Plato's Academy in Christian form. The group portrait projects a united and exceptionally gifted family. Old Judge John More holds an honoured position at his son's right hand. More's wife, Alice, and his daughters, hold books, indicating their learning. Musical, mathematical, and astronomical instruments are present in the room, indicating a breadth of interests. Later versions of the portrait include a dog and a pet monkey. The group is arranged in a semicircle as if gathered for morning prayer. But most members are busily occupied – no room for idleness or boredom here. This is a devout but learned Christian household, well ordered, living in harmony and peace, the perfect retreat for a busy statesman. Most significantly, the family represents the young and the old, the wise man and the fool, the richness and variety of human life, centred on commitment to God, source of all life.

The integration, rather than the separation, of human and religious activity, pleasure and morality, devotion and learning, was characteristic of humanism. Since this is how More wished to portray what he held to be most precious in his life, it would be helpful to examine More's Christian humanist thought and ideals, especially in relation to marriage, family, education and friendship.

In Defence of Humanism
Early Writings 1500–1519

Nothing is more humane – and humanity is the virtue most proper to human beings – than to relieve the misery of others, assuage their griefs, and by removing all sadness from their lives, to restore them to enjoyment, that is, pleasure. (THOMAS MORE: *UTOPIA* BOOK 2)

The modern word *humanism*, first coined in 1808 by a German scholar, was derived from a similar word *humanista* (Italian: *umanista*), used in the fifteenth and sixteenth centuries for professional university teachers of the five humanities (or liberal arts): grammar, rhetoric, poetry, history, ethics. Humanists, sometimes dubbed 'mere grammarians', were prepared to go back to the basics of the Greek and Latin languages so as really to understand, and enter the thought world of, the great classical writers of the past. By being in touch again with the best that human thought and action had achieved, they felt they could come to know what it was to be truly human, and put it into practice in their own lives. Humanists despised scholars who lived only on quotation or translation, because they were not equipped to read the complete text in the original language. Humanists wanted to read the whole text in its living context, not in isolation from it. For them, language was an expression of living experience.

The term 'humanist', initially restricted to the professional academic, came to be applied to many of their students who chose careers outside the university setting. These could be churchmen, royal councillors, secretaries to kings or city councils, schoolmasters, or interested lay men (rarely women) with time and leisure to study. More belonged to this network of lay humanists, who often had a distinctive contribution to make to civic and public life. These men had an interest in political thought and practical ethics as a guide to civic humanism. Their ideal of a 'sound classical education' as a preparation for public life, passed into the (English) public and grammar school systems, and dominated educational practice until our own century.

At its core humanism was neither religious nor irreligious, but most humanists were believing Christians and many were committed to the reform of Christendom. The rebirth (*renaissance*) of interest in classical sources came to include a rebirth of interest in biblical and early Christian sources, and a conviction that Christianity could be renewed only by returning to its roots. If the pagan classics put a person in touch with the best expression of what it was to be 'truly human', the Christian classics put one in touch with what it was to be 'truly Christian', rooted in the actual life of Jesus Christ himself. Humanists were concerned with integrating, not separating, the human and the Christian. They sought to deepen their understanding of both in a secular, not a cloistered, setting.

The teachers of the humanities and the new biblical theology increasingly challenged the teachers of theology, who used the older methods of the medieval academics (or scholastics). Their rival arguments about method and content in education became increasingly bitter and acrid. Humanists regarded speech as *the most characteristic human gift*. Knowledge remained private and sterile unless shared with another. To be able to communicate well was essential for the preacher or teacher, councillor or politician. It was not without significance that Christ, the supreme teacher, had been the *word* (or speech) *of God made human*. And his word moved human hearts. What was at stake for Christian humanists was the pastoral strategy needed to revitalize Christian thought and practice.

7

Humanism in its English context began earlier and continued later than has been supposed. The historian Denis Hay has drawn attention to the 'density of humanist activity in England'. There were many more humanists than one influential group operating in London. But it seems that while they were influential educators and editors of texts, they published no outstanding humanistic writings. Their hopes and promises were fulfilled in the lay amateur, Thomas More. Arguably the first two masterpieces of English renaissance humanism were his *History of King Richard III* (*c*.1513–1518), and *Utopia* (1516).

To understand More as a humanist expert in the art of speaking and writing well, with a preference for dialogue over systematic thought, provides the best interpretative framework for all his subsequent writings. More is urbane and witty in *Utopia*, vitriolic in his polemical writings, and devotional in his prison writings. Some scholars regard these differences as evidence for a deeply divided and ambiguous personality, bordering on imbalance. But a humanist was one trained in the art of using language and speech appropriate to the occasion. More could turn as easily to polemic as to eulogy, to satire and ridicule as to compassion, to earthy, bawdy Chaucerian farce as much as to other-worldly spirituality. This means that More's thought can never be separated from the context in which it was conceived. His thinking was at its best when interacting with people and concrete situations. His writings can only be understood in the light of his life and experience, and his life in relation to his writings.

'Learning Joined With Virtue': More's Household

More's vocation as a Christian humanist began in his home, and it was here that he first put his educational ideals into practice. A household in his time consisted not just of wife and children, but also of many attendants and servants. If we agree with the judgement that 'domestic hierarchy in late medieval England both reflected and reinforced political values' (LAWRENCE STONE), then More's home was also the foundation of his political and civic values. Youth was 'the seed-time on which the state depends for its future growth' (ERASMUS).

In many ways More's was a conventional Tudor patriarchal household, where a husband and father had almost unconditional rights over property, and had a duty to 'control' an unruly wife, children or servants. Stone points out that a father ruled his household much as a king ruled his court, and that both institutions were 'mutually supportive' in stressing the importance of docility, obedience, and respect for authority. More's may have been a fairly benign rule, and his preference for 'citizen' rather than 'subject' in the political order, is reflected in the love, equality and companionship he showed to members of his family. But rule it was; he was the undisputed head of the household.

More differed from his contemporaries in the importance he attached to the formal education of his children. Erasmus, as an observant visitor, saw More's household as a place of education:

> *You would say that in that place was Plato's Academy. But I do the house an injury in likening it to Plato's Academy. I should rather call it a school or university of Christian religion. For there is none therein who does not study the branches of a liberal education. Their special care is piety and virtue'.* (ERASMUS TO JOHN FISHER)

Piety and *virtue* are words which do not commend themselves to us today. For Erasmus, *piety* meant a loving, practical religion, and *virtue* meant the moral strength of an informed conscience, which could make good choices in the business of every-day life. But *virtue* also carried within it the old Roman, classical sense of 'virile energy', strength to stand up and shape destiny, rather than remain helpless or passive in the face of the inevitable. Again and again More's moralism included praise of *industry* and hatred of *idleness.* He declared he would give up public life rather than 'allow his children to be idle and lazy'. Idleness or inactivity was the bain of domestic, spiritual, intellectual or political life. Life at all these levels was something human beings could energetically create, in collaboration with the grace of God. 'We may not expect ... to get to heaven in feather beds', he declared when the going was tough; and a little later: 'God sent people here to wake and work' (CW 13). But the activity of play or pleasure was also a 'work'.

Erasmus and More shared an almost unlimited optimism about the power of education to shape mature, moral, industrious, religious persons, and to provide an antidote to the damaging effects of the 'original sin' of our first parents. A good education gave the best possible start 'for the whole scope of human life – which is to have a sound mind in a sound body' (SL 31). They also shared a perception of life lived in an upside-down world of human folly. Human beings were not so much sinful as foolish or stupid. Life was a comedy of errors, because so often people were taken in by appearances, empty promises, or flattery. Education was the chief means of acquiring true wisdom and avoiding folly. It was the 'natural' foundation upon which the grace of God could build.

More hired distinguished tutors for his 'school', which included others besides his own four children. His justly acclaimed interest in the education of woman was at least partly due to the accident that there were more girls than boys in his household and among family connections. He supervised every detail of their education, wrote to them during his absence from home, and expected them to write to him daily, as a kind of formal exercise. More's letters to one tutor, William Gonell (c.1518), express most clearly his hopes and fears for his children. He wants them to be able to

> put virtue in the first place, learning in the second, and in their studies to esteem most whatever may teach them piety towards God, charity to all and Christian humility in themselves. (SL 20)

He is pleased, he told Gonell, that Elizabeth has made so much progress, and that she has not allowed it to go to her head.

> *Let her understand that such conduct delights me more than all the learning in the world. Though I prefer learning joined with virtue to all the treasures of kings, yet renown for learning, if you take away moral probity, brings nothing else but notorious and noteworthy infamy, especially in a woman. Since erudition in a woman is a new thing and a reproach to the sloth of men, many will gladly assail it, and impute to learning what is really a fault of nature ... On the other hand ... if a woman, to eminent virtue of mind should add even a moderate skill in learning, I think she will gain more real good than if she obtain the riches of Croesus and the beauty of Helen ...* (SL 20)

The reward of wisdom depends on 'inner knowledge of what is right, not on the talk of men'. More is concerned with the formation of conscience, and with good judgement in ordinary life. 'Warn my children not to lament that they do not possess what they mistakenly desire in others; not to think more of themselves for gaudy trappings, nor less for the lack of them' (Rogers 129). He is afraid that if the children are praised too much for their efforts, they will become dependent on the good opinion of others and be easily deceived by flattery. So Gonell must be sparing with praise, and direct them to understand that 'the whole fruit of their endeavours should consist in the testimony of God and a good conscience'. Poor children, we might say, if we did not know that More also made learning fun for them: he taught them to read by shooting arrows at letters, and sought useful aids to memory, and methods to make study easier. And he found it hard to punish them except with the lightest tip of a peacock's tail.

Margaret grew up to become one of the most learned women of her day, informally accepted as a member of Erasmus' circle. Elizabeth, Cecily and John were also educated in Latin, Greek and science. Family prayer and religious education – a heavy diet of reading from the early Christian writers – were also part of the structured day. More's ideas on the education of women directly influenced the first important treatises on the subject: Juan Luis Vives' *On the Instruction of A Christian Woman* (1523) and Sir Thomas Elyot's *Defence of a Good Woman* (1540). (Elyot's wife had been one of the children at More's school.) More's experiment proved to his friends that women were as capable as men of benefiting from higher education. And though an educated wife was a good investment for a man, it was also important for the woman herself. More encouraged Margaret to continue her studies even after her marriage and the birth of her first child. Her role was not to be purely domestic. So in many ways More's views were innovative, creative and well ahead of his time.

More's early poetry contains some elegant tributes to women he admired: for example, 'An Apology to a certain noble lady', or 'He expresses his joy at finding her ... whom he had loved as a young boy'. The latter was a tender, almost romantic, poem, expressing regret at the passing of time and young love, but also its enduring power in the human memory. A 'Rueful Lamentation' (1503) was an elegy written on the occasion of the death of Queen Elizabeth of York, wife of Henry VII. More imagines Elizabeth regretting her untimely death and reluctant to leave her family. He allows a woman's voice to express the sadness of human mortality, and the inevitable separation from those we love.

More's views on women are ambivalent and contradictory. In the letter to Gonell cited above, he also suggests that though women are as capable as men of being educated, they actually need it more: 'A woman's wit is the more diligently to be cultivated, so that nature's defect may be redressed by industry'. Here More shares a common view within the Christian tradition, about the 'special' nature of women, who seem to be especially prone to foolishness or folly, because less amenable to reason. Education will help them not to follow their emotions, or indulge in trivial gossip or idleness. In an epigram, 'To Candidus: how to choose a wife', More advises him to be guided in his choice by reason, not considerations of beauty or money: 'Let her be either educated or capable of being educated', for learning can foster a sound judgement and self-knowledge. A good wife can become a source of goodness for others:

> Armed with this learning, she would not yield to pride in prosperity, nor grief in distress – even though misfortune strike her down ... If she is well instructed herself, then some day she will teach your little grandsons at an early age to read ... When she speaks, it will be difficult to judge between her extraordinary ability to say what she thinks and her thoughtful understanding of all kinds of affairs.

Those who have researched the images of women, real or fictional, in More's writings, have noted that while his early humanistic poems and letters present a positive attitude, the traditionally negative one lies very near the surface. More's 'modernity' frequently slips back into traditionalism. The anti-feminine discourse of the medieval sermon, or 'merry tale', is part of his inherited outlook. More loved to mock and ridicule, and women were often the special targets of his wit.

In his later polemical works, the vitriolic language meted out to his religious opponents is matched by his abusive language about women. In these writings women are likely to be seductive, idle, garrulous or foolish, and are generally inferior to men. As More saw it, 'unruly' or disordered women seem to reflect the disorder in the Church, or to embody danger in a very specific way. The exceptions are the good, no nonsense, articulate women, who hit the nail on the head by sheer common sense, and are a match for their men. These would seem to mirror Alice, his wife. His later Tower writings mark a return to civility and normality. When he was in prison, and with his life in danger, his beloved daughter Margaret begged him to conform and save himself by taking the required oath. He compared her to the 'temptress Eve'. She was not the usual, dutiful daughter; she argued with him and presented her case very ably. Despite the poignancy of their situation, he could be proud of her independence of mind.

It would seem that in all More's writings he spoke little about the institution of marriage, but much about the family as the foundation for a good society. It was assumed that husband and wife entered a life-long relationship for the sake of the family they were founding. Their joint responsibilities extended to all

> *that are belonging to our charge, by nature as our children, by law as our servants in our household. If servants fall sick in our service, so that they cannot do the service that we employ them for, we may still not in any way turn them out of doors and throw them aside comfortless, while they are unable to work and help themselves. For this would be a thing against all humanity.*
> (DC 2 17)

In another letter he wrote: 'Even if I do not leave myself a spoon, no poor neighbour of mine shall suffer any loss through any misfortune which happened in my house.' A well-ordered household reflected the principles of justice and equity, which should also be found in a well governed state.

More was to speak in wonder of the natural miracle of human coupling which resulted in gestation and birth. He remembered two young people in his own parish:

> *It happened, as it does among young people, that they fell in love and were married at St Stephen's. And within a year she gave birth to a fine boy ... I cannot understand why we should consider it more wonderful to revive a dead man than to witness the conception, birth and growth of a child into a man.* (CW6 1 79)

He also had a robust and earthy attitude to human sexuality, which may offend the pious or puritanical, but which most know to be fairly typical of his time and social class. More knew himself to be blessed in his family relationships, and he influenced a movement for the education of women. His humanistic ideals were sometimes overshadowed by his inherited attitudes about the nature of women and the role of the father in a Tudor household. But his ideals for the education of his children, his conviction that family life was the foundation of civic and political life, and that it embraced friends, neighbours and the less fortunate, have few recorded parallels within the long history of the Christian tradition.

In Defence of Humanism

More's interest in education extended beyond the family to higher and university education. He shared in the humanist struggle to reform educational practice, in which certain power groups had a vested interest. His ideas are most clearly expressed in four long letter-essays: to a theologian, Martin Dorp (1515), to Oxford University (1518), to a monk (1519), and to Edward Lee, future Archbishop of York (1519). Certain themes are common to all four letters, but in the first two More was directly intervening in the inter-faculty feuding at two universities; Louvain and Oxford. The feud was between the humanists (teachers of the liberal arts) and the scholastics (teachers of theology). The humanist-scholastic debates were a replay of the old classic Platonic debates about the respective merits of rhetoric and philosophy.

Martin Dorp, a member of the theological faculty at Louvain, was a 'lapsed' humanist, and so his criticism of Erasmus was all the more hurtful. In an exchange of letters, Dorp took Erasmus to task for undermining the authority of the Church in two ways: firstly, by undertaking his own translation of the New Testament, Erasmus would downgrade the old, authoritative text of Jerome's

Latin translation, known as the Vulgate. Secondly, in his *Praise of Folly*, Erasmus had ridiculed and made fun of people who held authority in the Church (monks, bishops, popes, rulers) whom, he said, acted from self-love, not charity. Criticism of either authoritative text or persons was dangerous and damaging. But Dorp had further reservations: pagan or secular studies were a threat to true piety, and rhetoric was too sophisticated for the simple message of the gospel. Humanists should stick to their linguistic skills and not presume to move into the area of the professional theologian. What was at stake was the nature of 'true theology' and who was qualified to practise the discipline.

More, a layman outside the academic forum, wrote to Dorp in defence of Erasmus, and of the whole humanistic enterprise. He tried to do so more in sorrow than anger, and in a way which would persuade, rather than alienate, those for whom Dorp was a spokesman. His long letter (forty-seven pages) seems to have brought Dorp back into line. More argued very forcibly that those who went back to the original Greek text could improve on the accuracy of Jerome's Latin Vulgate. A knowledge of Greek (and if possible Hebrew) was an indispensable tool for biblical studies. Indeed, he wrote, linguistic skills were a better preparation for penetrating the meaning of revelation contained in the biblical text than the debating skills of the scholastic theologian.

More argued for a return to 'positive theology', by which he meant a simpler, more reflective, pastoral theology which had been used by the early Fathers of the Church. A true theologian was one who could comment and preach on the biblical texts, so that hearts could be moved and lives transformed. True theology was based on a loving appropriation of the texts which, by constant familiarity, came to colour one's whole life. This was quite a different approach to that of an academic, who used texts as a source for the defence of a doctrinal position. Dialectical skill had its place in argument and debate. In fact 'dialectic and rhetoric [are] as closely akin as fist and palm, since dialectic infers more

16

concisely what rhetoric sets out more elaborately' (CW 15 17). But in the matter of moving and persuading Christians to deeper faith and practice, the extended palm of friendship was to be preferred to the clenched fist of disputation and argument. Hence the new humanist method in theology was to be preferred to the medieval approach, and the persuasive power of ordinary language was preferable to the academic jargon of the scholastic theologian.

In 1518 More wrote to the Senate of the University of Oxford, intervening to solve similar tensions and difficulties. A group of Oxford theologians had begun to call themselves 'Trojans', indicating their opposition to Greek, and to the liberal arts. More had heard that the leader of these Trojans had chosen, during a lenten sermon, 'to blather all too liberally not only against Greek learning and stylistic refinement in Latin, but against all the liberal arts' (CW15 135). More appealed to the university authorities to end such factions and encourage all learning, including Greek. He reminded them of the progress being made at Cambridge, 'which you have always outshone', and asked them to restore peace. A university racked by contention will not prosper.

In these letters (1515–1519) More made a vigorous defence of pagan or secular learning. Christian humanists tried to give their answer to the age-old question of Tertullian (c.200): 'What has Athens to do with Jerusalem?' For them human nature and divine grace were in harmony, in that the human search for excellence was an integral part of the Christian search for holiness. Humanists opposed two powerful 'anti-intellectual' trends in sixteenth-century Christianity. Firstly, there was a *spiritual* tradition of 'holy ignorance' which believed that a simple, faithful soul was taught by the Holy Spirit and had need of no other teacher. Secondly there was a *theological* tradition which separated the 'supernatural' activities of faith from the 'natural' activities of reason. In fairness to More's scholastic opponents, they were not against human reason (anti-intellectual) since they valued classical philosophy very highly; but they disliked pagan poetry, literature and history.

Philosophy was useful for Christian theology; the rest was not. So More was defending human culture as expressed in the liberal arts against the 'barbarian' theologians, who thought such learning was at best an irrelevance, and at worst actually harmful.

But for More a major task of a Christian was 'the business of learning the best way to live in the world'. Christian belief had to be translated into every-day practice. 'It is a thing of less labour to know what they should believe, and to believe it when they know it, than it is to work well,' More argued against Tyndale. To know something about human life in all its complexities was important for every Christian and every theologian. This was the context in which faith was operative. The common experience of human beings was most poignantly and eloquently expressed in literature, poetry and history. The study of such writings was not a pretentious distraction, but rather allowed human wisdom to become a sure foundation for Christian wisdom and insight.

The History of Richard III: A Study in Tyranny

In his letter to Dorp, More had asserted that the foundation of theology is a knowledge of human nature and the human situation 'which apart from poets and orators can be best learned from historians'. More was interested in the springs of human motivation and behaviour. One subject was beginning to take hold of his political imagination: tyranny as the corruption of good government. It had already been addressed in several of his Latin poems, and was to recur again in his future thought, and in the dramatic events of his own life. Erasmus wrote that More 'always had a special loathing for tyranny and a great fancy for equality'. In about 1513 More began to work on *The History of King Richard III*, a version of events which had taken place in London in 1483 when he was a boy, and which were still fresh in the memory of Londoners. We now recognize that *Richard III* was in the process of being written, but lay unfinished, as More turned to write his classic work on

The Best State of a Commonwealth and The New Island of Utopia (1515). *Richard III*, a study in tyranny or the corruption of good government, is the dark underside of the ideal of good government proposed in *Utopia*. How human beings acquire the one, and avoid the other, was the core of his political thought and action.

Once again More was interested less in the abstract principles of good and bad government than in concrete examples of both. He had them ready to hand. Richard was an example of a king who was knowingly and deliberately unjust. He was a tyrant because he usurped power, and because he subsequently acted unjustly. More's version of the events of 1483 has been criticized for its historical inaccuracies; but he reconstructed the popular London account, and knew personally some of the participants in the drama, such as Archbishop Morton. *Richard III* is a study of how a country, blessed with good government under Edward IV, slipped quickly into bad government because of the ambitions of one man. Richard's predecessor, Edward, had not been innocent; he had also usurped the throne and had blood on his hands (the murder of Henry VI). But experience had taught him to bring wise government out of its dubious origins. Edward died leaving his country in peace, but warning all parties that this could be lost.

Richard set out to seize the throne from his nephews, the legitimate heirs. In a series of calculated steps he dismantled the legitimacy of their claims (by declaring them bastards), denied their right to the protection of sanctuary, or to their mother's household, and their right to the loyalty of their subjects. Richard sought and eventually secured the compliance of the nobles, clergy and judges – those whose job it was to uphold civic liberties. Initially tyranny had to try to assume the trappings of legitimacy, while those who suspected what was happening had to be quietly eliminated.

The key question raised within the dramatic dialogue of *Richard III* is: what does an individual do when he or she witnesses the erosion of civil and ecclesiastical liberties? More suggested that most remain passive and do nothing:

> *And so they said that these matters be but kings' games, as it were*
> *stage plays, and for the most part played upon scaffolds, in which*
> *poor men be but onlookers. And they that be wise will meddle no*
> *farther. For they that sometimes step up and play with them,*
> *when they cannot play their parts, they disorder the play and do*
> *themself no good.*   (HR3 83)

The poor have no power to influence events, and the wise think it
best to keep a low profile. More's metaphor of the stage/scaffold
brilliantly illustrates how the stage of public life can so often turn
into a scaffold for a political victim. He exposed the double standards of political life: Edward's mistress, Jane Shore, had to do public penance for having lived openly with the king, while Richard's
dark deeds of murder were committed in private and went unpun-
ished. She was disgraced, he was honoured.

Why did More select this subject in 1513? He shared with other
humanists a keen perception of the driving ambitions of renaissance princes, who spent much money on flamboyant lifestyles,
and ambitious wars of self-glory, while neglecting their real
responsibilities. When Henry VIII succeeded his father in 1509,
the new reign raised many hopes. Four years later these hopes
were proving illusory. So More began his reflections on the nature
of good and bad government, and the misuse of power. He drew on
his knowledge of the great classics of political thought: Plato's
Republic, Cicero's *De Officiis* and Augustine's *City of God*.

Good government must include respect for the life and liberty of
the subject and for the legal, civic and ecclesiastical liberties of the
realm. What happens when good government is threatened or
breaks down? We would love to know More's answer, but he never
finished his manuscript, which ends as Archbishop Morton moves
to take action against Richard. (The traditional view is that
church or state authorities have the right and duty to remove a
tyrant by force.) But by 1515/16, More was considering entering
the king's service; so a treatise on how to rid the nation of a prince

who had overstepped his rights was hardly politic. By that time he was working out another answer in *Utopia*. The philosopher or wise man must neither remain a passive spectator of events, nor use force to change them:

> *But there is another philosophy, more practical for statesmen, which knows its stage, adapts itself to the plot, and performs its role neatly and appropriately.*   (U BOOK 1)

If you cannot change events, then at least work to make them less harmful than they might have been.

In a very real sense *Utopia* provides the answer to the unfinished dilemma posed at the end of *Richard III*. More could not continue to air his misgivings in a historical narrative, which looked like repeating itself in contemporary events. He had to find another mode of discourse and a less provocative way to continue his reflections on the nature of good and bad government. And so *Utopia* was conceived: an imaginary island, perhaps somewhere in the New World, where citizens had arrived at a form of government which put Christian Europe to shame.

3

Utopian Vision
1515–1516

Our own age and ages to come will discover in his [More's] narrative, a seedbed, so to speak, of elegant and useful concepts from which men will be able to borrow. (WILLIAM BUDE, 1517)

In May 1515 More was sent to Flanders as part of a diplomatic delegation, probably in connection with the English-Flemish wool trade. The delegates met in Bruges, but negotiations were adjourned in late July. As More did not return to London until 25 October, he had three months of unexpected leisure at his disposal, so he began to set down his thoughts on the nature of good government, and the role of a good councillor. Having some business in Antwerp, he took the opportunity to meet Peter Giles, city clerk to the town council, and humanist friend of Erasmus. More and Giles clearly enjoyed each other's company, and their conversations formed the factual background to the fictional setting of More's embryonic book. With the help of his friends, More soon found a novel and creative way of entering into contemporary humanist debates on what constituted good government, and what was the price to be paid for entering public service.

Introducing *Utopia*

Antwerp was a major European port, crowded with ships and travellers from the New World, which had been discovered by Columbus less than twenty-five years earlier (1492). One day

Peter Giles supposedly introduced More to a Portuguese traveller, Raphael Hythloday, recently returned from the Americas. They were invited back to More's house. 'There in the garden we sat down on a bench covered with grassy turf, to talk together.' Their day-long conversations formed the setting and subject matter of *Utopia*, with an interlude for dinner between Book One and Book Two.

The longer name for More's new book was *The Best State of a Commonwealth and the New Island of Utopia*. Because the title has been shortened to *Utopia*, many readers have focused on the fictitious island of Book Two, and paid less attention to the real island – sixteenth-century England – described in Book One. But both books are equally important; to focus on the second is to miss the point. *Utopia* (meaning Nowhere) was in many ways a mirror image of a very real place: Tudor England. By creating a hypothetical world which could be set against the actual world, More hoped to stimulate thought and provoke debate and discussion. *Utopia*, thus conceived, was a realistic tool for political change and reform, and not idealistic (or Utopian) at all.

We now know that Book Two was probably composed first, and while More was in Flanders; Book One was completed on his return to England. More sent a copy of the completed work to Peter Giles, with an explanatory letter, which is probably the best guide to the author's enigmatic intentions. *Utopia*, written in Latin for a European readership, was first published in Louvain in December 1516, and was so well received that it was reprinted in Paris (1517) and in Basle (1518 two impressions). After the 1518 edition, there was to be a curious gap of over thirty years, before it was translated into English (1551). This undoubtedly reflected the difficult period of the early Reformation, when such a work, inviting critical reform, could be misunderstood in Catholic circles.

Though there is no substitute for reading the text of *Utopia* itself, opinion is so divided about its meaning and purpose, that a brief guide to conflicting interpretations may be helpful. One view is that *Utopia* should be read at its face value, and expresses More's blueprint for an ideal state. An alternative view is that *Utopia* is a highly enigmatic, ironic discourse, which partly expresses More's ideal and partly does not. This view is supported by those who would locate More's thought within broader humanistic concerns. *Utopia*, they would argue, is a trip to 'nowhere' (the Greek *ou* + *topos*), narrated by Hythloday, whose name means 'expert in nonsense'. So *Utopia* is partly More's ideal, and partly a model which he recognizes has severe limitations. A further view is that *Utopia* was a *jeu d'esprit*, something tossed off by More, and never intended to be taken seriously. This is the least convincing of the three approaches.

Book One: The Dialogue of Counsel

The fictitious setting for *Utopia* is a garden in Antwerp, where two friends, Morus and Peter Giles, come together to hear about Raphael Hythloday's travels. (More, the author, must be distinguished from his semi-fictional persona, Morus.) Hythloday is no ordinary traveller, but a man in search of the truth about political life, comparing the customs of one country with another. The friends are so impressed with the knowledge he has acquired as a 'political' tourist, that they press him to consider entering the service of a prince, and using his gifts as a good councillor. So almost immediately the friends are diverted from their main purpose – hearing an account of Hythloday's travels – into how he can best use his expertise back in Europe. Hythloday presents a strong case for not entering public life, since its business affairs disturb the tranquillity and leisure of mind necessary for thought – the highest form of activity open to human beings. Morus presents the case for such an engagement, since he considers the highest human activity is to be able to put one's gifts at the service of others for the common good.

Humanists were frequently called upon to give political advice to rulers. So they often discussed the topic of good counsel under two aspects. Firstly, how can a ruler secure good advice and distinguish true from false friends? Secondly, how can a philosopher engage in politics without loss of integrity and loss of that 'leisure' time necessary for thought? There were further pragmatic considerations: does good advice actually affect any policy directly? Do rulers ever take advice which goes against their self-interest? Is it better to concentrate power in the hands of a single ruler, or to share power among an elected group of magistrates? Does the common good ultimately depend on the kind of government which is in place? In discussion on *The Best State of a Commonwealth*, humanists drew heavily on classical political philosophy, especially the thought of Plato, Aristotle and Cicero. They were in agreement about what constituted the best state: one which had just laws, promoted the common good, and enabled its citizens to live well, happily and with human dignity. They differed about the means best suited to achieve this end. *Utopia* is concerned with all these questions.

In Book One of *Utopia*, Peter Giles speaks rarely. In its uneven dialogue Hythloday (the idealist) argues for non-involvement in public life, Morus (the realist) for involvement. Hythloday describes a supposed visit he made to England and a meal in the household of Archbishop Morton of Canterbury. Morton's 'table talk' turned to urgent issues in contemporary England: the widespread use of hanging for minor theft, which was both unjust and ineffectual; the number of crippled war veterans who swelled the ranks of beggars; the parasitic lifestyles of nobles living off the labour of others; the menace of nobles and retainers trained for war; the cruelty of enclosures forced by those who saw sheep as more profitable than smallholders or villagers; the disparity between the extravagantly rich and the destitute poor. In contemporary England individuals were motivated by self-interest, not by justice or equity. It was an example not of the best, but of the worst state of a commonwealth. When Hythloday tried to offer good advice, it fell on deaf ears. He was not attracted to the role of being a permanent councillor.

Following this trenchant social analysis of the state of contemporary England, Morus reminds Hythloday that Plato taught that commonwealths would be happy only when philosophers became kings or kings became philosophers. 'No wonder we are so far from happiness when philosophers do not condescend even to assist kings with their counsels' (U 28). Hythloday replies by imagining himself to be present at two kinds of royal councils. For example, were he to be present at the council of the king of France, could he dissuade him from pressing his claims to Milan, or Naples, or Flanders or Burgundy? Could he prevent the sham diplomacy and offers of peace which really served royal war aims? If he were to join another royal council (England thinly disguised), could wise counsel prevent unjust and manipulative ways of raising taxes, or stop judges from declaring in the interest of the king? Such councils are dishonourable and immoral. There is no place for the philosopher at the council of kings. A true philosopher must remain aloof from the corrupt world of politics.

Morus disagrees: there may not be a place for the academic philosophy of the schools in public life, but there is a place for a more practical, applied philosophy, which accommodates itself to the task at hand. Any society, including contemporary England, has less than desirable features. But you have to work with what you have, since politics is the art of the possible.

That's how things go in the commonwealth and in councils of princes. If you cannot pluck up bad ideas by the root, or cure long-standing evils to your heart's content, you must not therefore abandon the commonwealth. Don't give up the ship in a storm because you cannot direct the winds. And don't force strange and untested ideas on people who you know are firmly persuaded the other way. You must strive to influence policy indirectly, urge your case vigorously but tactfully, and thus what you cannot turn to good you may at least make as little bad as possible. For it is impossible to make everything good unless all men are good, and that I don't expect to see for quite a few years yet. (U 36)

Hythloday again argues the opposite case; accommodation to existing reality will not work. The moral (*honestas*) is not compatible with the expedient (*utilitas*):

When you say I should 'influence policy indirectly' I simply do not know what you mean ... In a council there is no way to dissemble or play the innocent. You must openly approve the worst proposals and warmly urge the most vicious policies. A man who went along only half-heartedly would immediately be suspected as a spy, perhaps a traitor. (U 37)

Hythloday continues: good government is impossible unless the evils of money and private property are rooted out, and people hold all things in common. Drastic remedies are required if things are really to change. A good state can be judged by what its citizens admire, or what conduct they think most deserving of praise and honour. Contemporary England operates on a false scale of social values. People attach enormous prestige to noble birth, wealth and its trappings, living in magnificent and showy splendour. A nobility trained for chivalry, thinks it honourable to go to war, or to pursue martial arts, or to hunt down animals for a pastime. The root of all these evils is private property and self-interest. And the riches of the few condemn the vast majority to a life of unrelieved poverty and unhappiness.

But things can be done differently. Hythloday has seen a society where there is no private property, where wealth is distributed evenly and citizens live in peace and happiness. He has seen this at work in the island of *Utopia*. His disbelieving friends suggest they adjourn for lunch before hearing any more.

It has been well argued that one of the multi-layered meanings of *Utopia* is pride as the source of social evil. Pride 'is not just feeling good about yourself. It is feeling good because you feel *superior* to someone else' (OLIN, *INTERPRETING THOMAS MORE'S* UTOPIA 41). Pride feeds on the envy or adulation of others. It needs the trappings of wealth, power, and position. It spawns the time-server and the flatterer. Pride is the special temptation of the ruler, who is not satisfied with the land he possesses, but undertakes wars of self-aggrandizement for dynastic reasons, bringing untold misery to others. Pride is the source of social sin, the political aspect of humanity's fall from grace. White argues that the central theme of Book One is this connection between pride and social evil (the problem), and that Book Two suggests how this evil might be eliminated (the solution). This is the essential connection between both books and the reason for the long digression of Book One.

Book Two: The New Island of Utopia

Hythloday's travel tale makes use of the intense contemporary excitement and public interest in the 'discovery' of the New World (1492). He supposedly made the outward journey with Amerigo Vespucci (1504), but stayed behind for some years of further travels. He arrived at *Utopia*, and was an open-minded observer of another culture. Hythloday describes a community of human beings untouched by either pagan classical civilization or Christian religion. Yet through their use of human intelligence and ingenuity, they had not only arrived at an advanced state of civilization, but held highly developed beliefs in God, providence, morality, and the immortality of the soul. Rational religion and philosophy were able to shape a just and equitable society, in many ways more advanced and admirable than contemporary Christian Europe. Utopian fiction was another way of expressing humanist belief that human beings had the power to shape their destiny, and had options open to them. Life was not a fate to be endured, but a future to be created, and in this, most of all, human beings resembled their creator, God.

GEOGRAPHY OF UTOPIA

Utopia is imagined as an island which, geographically and socially, is a mirror image of England. Its founder, Utopus, ordered a channel fifteen miles wide to be cut to separate the island from the mainland – and from contamination from the outside world. Utopia has fifty-four city states, and a capital, Amaurot, where three representative citizens from each city meet once a year. Every town is situated within at least a twelve-mile radius of farm land. Citizens have to work at least two years in a farming household on a rotating basis. (This is in direct contrast to Europe, where manual labour was held in contempt.) Rural households number forty or more adults, and are organized into groups of thirty, under a leader. The groups are self-sufficient, and either barter or share their surplus goods with their neighbours.

Amaurot, the capital, is a walled city on a tidal river, with an arched stone bridge (like London). Amaurot and all cities are carefully planned. The citizens enjoy piped water, good defences, wide streets, open doors and large gardens. 'In a sense gardens are symbolic of *Utopia* itself, a means of modifying the harm done in an earlier lost garden, and the delight taken in them is an anticipation of paradise regained', (*MORE'S UTOPIA*, 1991, D. BAKER-SMITH 160). Every ten years citizens exchange houses and gardens, as there is no privately owned property. Citizens are good tenants rather than property owners. Houses are comfortable, three-storeyed, faced with brick or stone, well decorated, and with glass or oiled linen in the windows.

Thomas More

GOVERNMENT

The Utopian form of government is a federation of cities which manage their own internal affairs. The basic group is the household. Once a year each group of thirty households elects a leader, and each group of ten such leaders elects its own representative (a tranibor). Only the tranibors may be re-elected. When needed, all elected officials come together, to choose a magistrate or governor from four men nominated by each area of the city. The governor holds office for life, unless 'suspected of aiming at tyranny', when he can be removed. The tranibors consult daily with the governor, and each time bring two different leaders with them to the senate. All matters of importance are discussed with a general assembly of elected officials, who also consult their households. Utopian city government tries to avoid an aristocracy, and to involve citizens in decision-making on democratic lines. But it is decidedly 'paternal', which reflects More's own family values. Governor, senate, and representative assembly relate in ways designed to block both tyranny and plotting factions. Strangely, in *Utopia* there is no positive enjoyment of politics; political structures exist to facilitate the 'good life', but are not really part of it.

OCCUPATIONS

Each citizen has two occupations: farming, which all must share in turn, and a choice of crafts or trades. Women work at lighter crafts, and sons usually follow their father's trade. Each citizen works for six hours a day, three before noon, and three after a siesta. Spare time is given over to intellectual pursuits. They have a period of recreation after supper for music or conversation, but they never gamble. They go to bed early, sleep eight hours, and rise early for public lectures before daybreak. (Commentators have noted the quasi-monastic structure of the Utopian day, and its resemblance to More's own household regime.)

Short working hours provide amply for their needs, as they do not have to provide luxury goods or inessentials. Some leaders may be exempt from work but often choose not to be. Scholars are exempted, and from this intellectual class are chosen the ambassadors, priests, tranibors and the governor himself. Only the learned may hold high public office, but in case they become a privileged group, their number is limited to about five hundred. Buildings last a long time and are kept in good repair. Back in Europe clothes locate a person socially, and are an indicator of rank and wealth. But the Utopians opt for the equality of uniform clothing, and use simple undyed fabrics (wool and linen), avoiding extravagance and waste.

SOCIAL AND BUSINESS RELATIONS, TRAVEL

Households are patriarchal, under the rule of the oldest male, and are limited to between ten and sixteen adults. On marrying, a woman joins the household of her husband. If a city exceeds six thousand households, it plants a new colony, preferably in uncultivated and unoccupied land. If the population shrinks, citizens are brought back from the colonies. *Utopia* is not a money economy. Heads of households collect what they need from area markets. Families dine in common dining halls assigned to each ward of the city, thirty families to each hall. Their women take it in turns to prepare meals, and nurses and infants are assigned a separate area. Stewards collect the food for halls and local hospitals. Citizens serving penal time as slaves do the chores and heavy work. The leader and his wife sit at a high table, with two elders or the priest. Seating is arranged in fours, with young and old interspersed. Children and unmarried young people either wait at table, or wait for food to be given them by adults. In remote rural households, meals are taken at home.

Citizens may only travel to other districts with permission, and must earn their own keep. There are no wine-bars, ale-houses, brothels or spots for secret meetings: they live in full view of all. If they make a trade surplus abroad, it is kept against a contingency such as war. They do not prize gold or silver but use them to make chamber pots, humbler vessels, and even the chains and fetters of slaves. Gems are used as playthings for children until they know better. Visiting ambassadors, who wear ostentatious dress and jewels, evoke surprise and ridicule, rather than honour and respect. In general, Utopians are amazed to meet people who value others for their wealth or dress, rather than their virtue. Both their way of life and their study confirm these views.

PHILOSOPHY: IN PRAISE OF PLEASURE

In the descriptive opening narrative of Book Two, Hythloday is not trying to describe the maximum desirable features of this state, but rather the minimum *necessary* for the happiness of its citizens. Even so, certain physical, constitutional or economic choices must be made to attain even minimum goals, and there is the recognition that even in the best state there may be conflict between valid goals. This may explain, or make sense of, some puzzling aspects of the work: the fact that More's commonwealth is a flawed one, and in places at variance with his own ideals.

Utopia is imagined as an inclusive society based on collective security, rather than on inequality of fortune founded on individual endeavour. However, it becomes clear that the equality, which guarantees satisfaction of basic needs and time for leisure, is very restrictive of personal liberty and choice. *Utopia* may be highly moral, but it is also exceedingly dull and uniform. And yet these people who live 'according to nature' are in essentials Epicureans (lovers of pleasure) rather than Stoics (those who make virtue the highest good). They discuss the nature of both virtue and pleasure, but their chief concern is *human happiness, and whether it consists of one thing or many. They seem rather too much inclined to the view that all or the most important part of human happiness consists of pleasure. And what is more surprising, they seek support for this comfortable opinion from their religion ... for they never discuss happiness without joining to their philosophic rationalism certain principles of religion. Without these religious principles they think that reason is bound to prove weak and defective in its efforts to investigate true happiness.* (U 67–8)

There is an opposed school in *Utopia* which argues that virtue itself is happiness, whether it leads to pleasure or not. They say virtue means living according to nature.

Nothing is more humane (and humanity is the virtue most proper to human beings) than to relieve the misery of others, assuage their griefs, and by removing all sadness from their lives, to restore them to enjoyment, that is pleasure. Well, if this is the case, why doesn't nature equally invite us to do the same thing for ourselves? ... Thus, they say, nature herself prescribes for us a joyous life, in other words pleasure, as the goal of our actions; and living according to her rules is to be defined as virtue. And as nature bids men to make one another's life cheerful ... so she repeatedly warns you not to seek your own advantage in ways that cause misfortune to others ... she cherishes alike all those living beings to whom she has granted the same form. (U 70)

Utopia is an attempt to create a society and culture where the pursuit of pleasure (self-interest) and virtue (consideration for others) are not mutually exclusive. Utopians believe that the goal of life, or happiness, consists mainly in the cultivation of the mind, and depends on domestic order and freedom from conflict. The enjoyment of pleasurable activities (in moderation) is compatible with virtue. But in *Utopia* the rational devices used to curb and control human ambition and greed screen out much of the variety, richness and unpredictability of human living. The state knows best how to provide for education, training, communal goods, family and civic life. It is a uniform, grey civilization, and perhaps reflects More's pessimism, that it is not really possible to create a 'good' society on earth.

Paradoxically, however, Utopian communism is close to the spirit of the early Church, where Christians held all things in common, 'and had but one mind and one heart' (ACTS 4:32). 'If the entire second book has a symbol, it is that of the common dining hall which abounds in good things and pleasures. Each meal taken together stands for the triumph of justice and equity, and represents the equality and communion of all the citizens' (E. SURTZ, CW, *UTOPIA*, XXV). To us the lack of privacy and freedom of choice seems contrary to our notions of human dignity. But the sixteenth-century household knew little privacy, and even less about individual (as opposed to communal) entitlement and rights.

Utopian practices are to be preferred to many features of contemporary Europe. Utopians dislike ostentatious dress, and cannot understand those who are taken in by flattery, empty ceremony or honours. They count these, as well as gambling, dicing and hunting, as false pleasures.

> *If what you want is slaughter, if you want to see a living creature torn apart before your eyes, then the whole thing is wrong. You ought to feel nothing but pity when you see the hare fleeing from the hound, the weak creature tormented by the stronger, the fearful and timid beast brutalized by the savage one, the harmless hare killed by the cruel hound.* (U 73)

There is pity for animals here, but also a hatred for pastimes which are considered honourable by the European nobility, but which brutalize, and are a form of training for the martial arts.

CONTROVERSIAL FEATURES OF UTOPIAN SOCIETY

Utopian society has slaves, either taken as prisoners of war, or citizens deprived of freedom for their crimes. Utopians are not born into slavery, and so there is no 'slave class' by birth or nature (an improvement on classical times). Sometimes foreign criminals condemned to death in another country, or foreign vagrants, are imported as slaves. Slaves are not essential but rather convenient to the economy, as they perform the lowliest tasks such as butchery. Slavery is a punishment for a severe and public crime. 'Slaves are permanent and visible reminders that crime does not pay ... But if they are patient they are not left without hope' (U 82). Their sentences can be commuted, although rebellion means instant death.

Though the sick are well cared for, the priests and public officials encourage the terminally ill to consider ending their own lives.

> *They never force this step on a man against his will; nor if he decides against it, do they lessen their care of him. The man who yields to their arguments, they think, dies an honourable death; but the suicide, who takes his own life without the approval of priests and senate, they consider him unworthy of either earth or fire, and throw his body, unburied and disgraced, into the nearest bog.* (U 81)

Though marriage is normally for life, and adultery severely punished, the Utopians allow divorce in rare cases, where it can be proved the marriage has broken down completely. Before marriage 'the bride-to-be is shown naked to the groom by a responsible and respectable matron; and similarly, some respectable man presents the groom naked to his prospective bride' (U 83). Though the custom seems absurd to the visitors, the Utopians regard it as essential to be legally protected from deception or physical deformity before the marriage takes place.

Utopians despise war 'and think nothing so inglorious as the glory won in battle'. They only go to war for good reasons: self-defence, to repel invasion, or to liberate an oppressed people. They dislike a victory won at too high a price. There is no standing army, but a civilian militia (including women) called up when needed. But some of their practices are highly dubious: to save their own citizens, they prefer to hire mercenaries; they use their surplus money, acquired by trading but not usable at home, to destabilize the enemy and reward hit killers; they enslave prisoners of war, take money and estates as war indemnities; they turn the inhabitants off land they conquer or need for colonies. Utopians do not regard foreigners as equals with civic rights, and their foreign policy is expedient rather than moral. So, although *Utopia* works well insulated from the outer world, contact through war or colonization brings a host of unsolved problems. (Does More intend his readers to pick this up and to realize that his ideal state had less than ideal features? He seems to leave these matters enigmatically open.)

RELIGION AND RELIGIOUS TOLERANCE

Utopians have moved from more primitive mythic religions to a form of rational deism. Different forms of religion are tolerated throughout the island but the vast majority of Utopians

> *believe in a single power, unknown, eternal, infinite, inexplicable, far beyond the grasp of the human mind, and diffused throughout the universe, not physically but in influence. They call him father, and to him alone they attribute the origin, increase, progress, change and end of all visible things; they do not offer divine honours to any other.* (U 96)

All citizens share in a similar form of public temple worship, and hold simple basic beliefs in common: a belief in the divine government of the world and in the immortality of the soul. Some religious diversity is allowed within the household rites. Utopians inherited a tradition of religious tolerance from their founder, who thought that:

> *even if one religion is really true and the rest false, the true one will sooner or later prevail by its own natural strength, if men will only consider the matter reasonably and modestly ... so he left the whole matter open allowing each person to choose what he would believe.* (U 98)

In such matters Utopus 'was not quick to dogmatize,

> *because he suspected that God perhaps likes various forms of worship, and has deliberately inspired different men with different views. On the other hand he was quite sure that it was arrogant folly for anyone to enforce conformity with his own beliefs by threats or violence.'*

Utopus even allowed a man to try to make converts, provided he did so 'quietly, modestly, rationally and without bitterness towards others. If persuasion failed, no man might resort to abuse or violence, under penalty of exile or slavery.' But it is a toleration within strict limits: anyone who denied the minimal basic beliefs in divine providence, or the immortality of the soul, was denied public office and held in disgrace. 'Yet they do not punish him, because they are persuaded that no man can choose to believe by a mere act of will ... and they are confident that in the end his madness will yield to reason' (U 99).

When Utopians heard about Christianity they were well disposed towards it, and many were baptized. But 'those who have not accepted Christianity make no effort to restrain others from it, nor do they criticize new converts to it' (U 97). An unruly, over-enthusiastic convert who 'created a public disorder', was exiled, not punished: 'it is one of their oldest rules that no one should suffer for his religion' (U 97).

In view of More's later controversial writings and intolerant attitude towards those who did not share his beliefs during the Reformation, it is important to grasp the social and civic limits to a Utopian form of religious toleration. A citizen who did not believe in God or an after-life was a civic threat, and had to be exiled from the community – but not physically punished. It is also of interest to see the Utopian priesthood as limited in number, inclusive of women, and characterized by great personal holiness. Priests exercise no power 'beyond that which derives from their good repute' (U 102). By implication, this is a criticism of worldly, powerful and corrupt clerics in Christian Europe, and expresses a desire for clerical reform.

Back to Reality: The Uses of *Utopia*

Hythloday (the idealist) finishes his praise of *Utopia* by comparing 'this justice of the Utopians with that which prevails among other nations', especially in Christian Europe. He ends where he began, listing the deeds of social injustice prevalent in contemporary society. 'When I run over in my mind the various commonwealths flourishing today ... I can see in them nothing but a conspiracy of the rich, who are fattening up their own interests under the name and title of the commonwealth' (U 108). The root cause is human pride. Morus (the realist) is very suspicious of the cure: Utopian communism. But Hythloday is tired – and inclined to be touchy. Morus tactfully guides him in to supper, and leaves his criticisms for another day.

How does More intend his readers to react to his Utopian fiction? Are we expected to share Hythloday's enthusiasm for a society based on common ownership? Or do we come away like Morus, impressed but convinced it is an impracticable dream?

Meanwhile, while I can hardly agree with everything he said ... yet I freely confess that in the Utopian commonwealth there are many features that in our own societies I would like, rather than expect, to see. (U 111)

Is More happy to have sown the seeds of possible ways of acting, and to leave it to his readers to decide whether some (or any) of them can be transplanted into the politics of the real world? If, in this real world, private property is retained (the indications are that More thought this to be inevitable), did he intend us to see that the price to be paid is very high? More intended Utopian society to be a reminder of the limitations we may have to place on unrestricted human freedoms, in the interests of the good of others, and of living in harmony in a community.

At almost exactly the same time, and unknown to More, his contemporary Niccolo Machiavelli was writing his famous political work, *The Prince* (1513). He wrote:

Many have imagined republics and principalities which have never been seen or known to exist in reality; for how we live is so far removed from how we ought to live, that he who abandons what is done for what ought to be done, will rather learn to bring about his own ruin than his preservation. (THE PRINCE)

More and Machiavelli would have agreed that 'how we live is ... far removed from how we ought to live' because human beings are essentially self-interested and self-regarding. But Machiavelli went on to state that the art and logic of acquiring and maintaining political power meant manipulating and using human self-interest. 'A man who wishes to make a profession of goodness in everything must necessarily come to grief among so many who are not good.'

This is precisely Hythloday's reason for not engaging in the corrupt world of politics. The moral (*honestas*) is incompatible with the expedient (*utilitas*). Hythloday wanted to retire from a life of public service to one of tranquil thought – unless self-interest can be neutralized, as in Utopian society. He opted for the moral. Machiavelli wanted to withdraw from 'making a profession of goodness in politics'. He opted for the expedient. More remained committed to a strategy which struggled to combine the moral and the expedient: for virtue and honesty in public life are their own reward. Politics is the art of the possible. A good man cannot abandon the public sphere, and those who need protection from injustice. By being there he can at least temper its severity: 'what you cannot turn to good, at least make as little bad as possible' (U 36).

The struggle to relate the moral and the expedient was to be severely tested at least twice in More's public life. What does a Lord Chancellor do when citizens refuse to obey willingly the laws against heresy? Is he morally justified in using force, even violence, to get compliance? And what happens to a loyal servant of the crown when he has to choose between the moral and the expedient – either refusing an immoral oath or conforming to the wishes of his prince? The issues raised theoretically in *Utopia* were to become real in More's own public and personal life.

4

The King's Servant
Public Life 1517–1532

*In your counsel-giving unto his grace, ever tell him what he ought
to do, but never what he is able to do ... For if a lion knew his own
strength, hard were it for any man to rule him.* (THOMAS MORE
TO THOMAS CROMWELL)

Thomas More was appointed to the King's Council sometime in
1517. He joined his father John, and his humanist friends, John
Colet and Cuthbert Tunstall, who were already members of the
council. He did not tell Erasmus for some time, and then gave him
to believe that he had accepted the office with some reluctance.
'No one has ever been so eager to get into court as More was
to stay out of it,' wrote Erasmus to a friend. But More's supposed
reluctance to assume office has been reassessed; we now believe
that though he did not accept office lightly, he chose it and
wanted it.

There was a high price to be paid. When More sent his finished
Utopia to his friend Peter Giles (1516), he complained in an
accompanying letter how difficult it was to find time to write :

*Most of my day is given to the law, pleading some cases, hearing
others ... I have to visit this man because of his official position and
that man because of his lawsuit; and so almost the whole day is
devoted to other people's business; and what's left over to my own;
and then for myself – that is my studies – there is nothing left.
For when I come home I must talk with my wife, chat with my*

children, and converse with my servants ... and this has to be done
unless one wants to be a stranger in one's own home. (U 4)

More concludes that he can only snatch time to write from ' the time stolen from sleep and food'. This situation could only get worse as he entered public life and assumed public responsibilities. Apart from a brief period in 1528–1529, More rarely had leisure for writing, reading or research. He did not merely observe, but was deeply involved in, the political issues of the day. Before assessing his polemical and devotional writings, this chapter will briefly consider the public context of his life which shaped, but also put quite exceptional constraints on, his literary output.

Councillor, Diplomat, Secretary (1517–1529)

Henry VIII disliked the routine of government, which he left to his councillors and to his chancellor, Wolsey. This meant that there were two centres of politics: this King's court in royal progress from one residence to another, and Wolsey's household operating from York House or Hampton Court. Wolsey effectively governed England, though he had to keep the King informed of state business, secure his signature for documents, and appear to defer to his will. Wolsey was rarely in attendance on the King, and lived in constant fear that resident courtiers would work to erode his influence and power. In such a situation it was essential to have councillors trusted by both King and Chancellor. More fulfilled this role with integrity and skill for twelve years, before his own appointment to the chancellorship.

In 1523 Wolsey pressed Henry VIII to give More a generous fee for services rendered, because 'he is not the most ready to speak and solicit his own cause'. In this More lived out his Utopian ideals. The real interest, however, lies in the question put in *Utopia*: can a wise councillor actually influence political events, or make any substantive contribution to public life, if he is unwilling to fight political battles and get his hands dirty? In practice, how did More balance the claims of the moral and the expedient?

At first Henry used More mainly for his humanist skills as a secretary, orator and diplomat. As an orator he welcomed foreign visitors to court, and as a diplomat he accompanied the King or the Chancellor on foreign missions, and took part in negotiations. But it would seem that he was an adviser rather than an influential shaper of foreign policy. Wolsey frequently used him as his direct intermediary with the King. When at court Henry often sent for More to discuss astronomy, geometry or theology, and More probably had a hand in preparing Henry's *Defence of the Seven Sacraments* against Luther (1521). More's contribution to court entertainment was so valued that he found it difficult to escape to spend time with his wife and family. But he had no illusions about the permanence of royal favour. When his son-in-law Roper was unduly impressed after the King's visit to their home in Chelsea, More remarked 'Son Roper, I may tell thee I have no cause to be proud thereof, for if my head could win him a castle in France ... it should not fail to go' (ROPER 208).

More was elected Speaker of the House of Commons in 1523, a task to tax his principles and political skill. The Speaker spoke for the Commons: its members expected him to be their spokesman and to defend their liberties. But the Speaker was also the king's servant, expected to manage the Commons and get his business through. In 1523 More had to commend heavy war taxation to the House, while defending its right to speak its mind freely. Through the voice of its Speaker, the House did not capitulate to royal bullying. More's legal duties continued. With the court in progress, he dealt with the bills of complaint brought to the king. At Westminster he sat as judge in the Court of the Star Chamber, and was active on various reform committees.

In July 1525 More was appointed Chancellor of the Duchy of Lancaster, which involved residence at Court, with intervals away on Duchy business. He emerges as a 'hardworking administrator, a peacemaker more concerned to get at the causes of violence in the countryside, that to inflict harsh punishments, a protector of the weak against the strong, and an astute lawyer who could cut through the mass of detail to the heart of the matter in hand' (EA 118, M. HASTINGS). The Chancellorship of the Duchy was to be an invaluable preparation for the Chancellorship of England. However, More had no expectation of this in 1525; on the contrary, he was aware that Wolsey had promoted him 'sideways', to an office with more status but less influence and less remuneration.

From 1527 onwards, the question of the King's divorce from Catherine of Aragon was to prove the single most intractable political problem of the coming years. But though the King's 'great matter' was worrying, in More's view the growing influence of imported Protestant writings was even more serious. His friends convinced him that his gifts and reputation as a writer could be of incalculable use in combating heresy. So in March 1528 More accepted a licence from Tunstall, now Bishop of London, to acquire and read Protestant writings in order to refute their contents. He partly withdrew from public life to devote himself to this task. These writings will be considered in the next chapter.

Chancellor of England (1529–1532)

In June 1529 More was asked by Wolsey to help to negotiate the Peace of Cambrai. Within a few months Wolsey himself fell from power (October 1529), and after an interval of several days More emerged as a compromise candidate for the office of Lord Chancellor. His relative lack of power, aversion to faction and intrigue, and proven suitability for the judicial work of the office, made him a more acceptable choice than other rival candidates. More hesitated to accept, but was ordered by Henry to do so, the King promising 'never to molest his conscience' in the matter of the royal divorce. Shortly after receiving the seal of office on 25/26 October 1529, More launched a bitter attack on all that Wolsey had stood for. Perhaps this was a public exercise in damage limitation, since Henry (through More) had to explain Wolsey's sudden departure. Yet this unexpected attack on his disgraced former master does More little credit.

More's term of office as Chancellor was short, difficult and enmeshed with events which were part of the emerging Protestant Reformation in England. According to his biographer Roper, More desired three goals for Christian Europe, or as he thought of it, Christendom: perpetual peace between kings, extermination of heresy, and a 'good conclusion' to the King's divorce case (ROPER 210). The fragile Peace of Cambrai lasted until 1538; extermination of heresy was to be pursued by More as writer and as enforcer of the law; the 'conclusion to the King's divorce' was to be politically and personally disastrous for More. Inevitably More's views on universal Christendom clashed with the evolving ideas on the nature of a nation state, sovereign in all matters, spiritual and temporal. And More's (private) views on the royal divorce cast him as the political opponent of the king he tried to serve. 'The wonder is surely not that More ultimately failed but that he ever believed he might succeed' (GUY, *THE PUBLIC CAREER OF SIR THOMAS MORE*, 112).

More and the Law: Equity and Justice

More spent a great part of his life practising as a common lawyer and judge. 'It was as a judge, not as a politician, that his reputation stands highest' (GUY 93). When he became Lord Chancellor, More held the highest law office in the land, and in thirty-one months made a distinguished contribution to the development of impartial justice in the English legal system. Unfortunately he did not write a treatise either on English common law or on church canon law. Many of his own personal papers were either lost or confiscated. However, what he thought about either system of law, and its application to particular circumstances, including his own, is crucial for any appreciation of More as a Christian thinker. It has to be gleaned from his other writings, from court records, and from what we know of his life.

Roper gives us some insight into More's thought and practice. When More was Chancellor, some common law judges came to him, complaining that he was too free in issuing injunctions from the Chancery, which overruled their court judgements. More invited them to dinner, listened to their complaints, and offered a compromise: if, after thought, and acting on their own discretion, they could 'mitigate and reform the rigour of the law themselves', he would issue no more injunctions. When they refused his offer he declared he had no alternative but to continue to issue injunctions 'to relieve the people's injury' (ROPER 221).

As is evident from *Utopia* Book One, where Hythloday is critical of the entire English system of justice, More thought that the strict application of the common law to particular cases was often unjust and unfair. 'Extreme justice should properly be called extreme injury' (U 22, CITING CICERO). For example, using the death penalty for theft was unjust because disproportionate to the nature of the crime. It was also ineffectual, since it failed to deter. Those who enforced the law rarely considered the root causes of crime. Yet many people were driven to steal in order to survive, since society provided them with no alternative. If in turn their children grew up to be thieves, society (not malice) was to blame for making them criminals. The strict application of the law, irrespective of the social causes of crime, 'may look superficially like justice, but is in reality neither just nor practical' (U 21). Hythloday (More) challenged the 'law and order' school of thought, which regarded punishment as a debt the criminal owned to society, but never looked at what society owed to the criminal: moral and social rehabilitation (U 24).

More was convinced that the administration of English justice was often slow, cumbersome, and biased in favour of the rich, who could afford lengthy litigation. The criminal laws were like 'cobwebs, in which the little nits and flies stick still and hang fast, but the great bumblebees break them and fly quite through' (D 230). Much of English law was case law, not framed in universal terms, but relying on the precedents of previous judgements. It often involved very rigid procedures, which needed to be simplified and processed more quickly. Judges also needed to be guided by the spirit of equity (the desire to be fair) and to balance the spirit against the letter of the law.

The tendency for common lawyers to stick to the strict application of the rigid procedures of the common law, was checked by the growth of new equity courts (the Star Chamber and Chancery), especially under the Tudors. More's predecessors as chancellor, Archbishops Morton, Wareham and Wolsey, all felt that the common law was too inflexible and failed to respond to changing circumstances. They used the Chancellor's Court, which had no jury, to cut through the technicalities of the common law and give justice more swiftly. More did not so much innovate as extend their practice, by making still greater use of these courts of equity. The prospect of making justice more available to the poor probably attracted him to working with Wolsey in the first place.

In 1528 a distinguished common lawyer, Christopher Saint German, began to develop his arguments for greater use of the principle of equity, in a treatise later expanded and published under the title *Doctor and Student*. What we know of More's thought and practice indicates his broad agreement with Saint German on the equity principle. (They were to agree on little else, as we shall see.) Saint German argued that too much attention to the procedures of the law tends to legalism, and can obscure common sense and ordinary fair-mindedness. He wanted to reorder and reform the rather messy and diverse traditions of the common law, and to re-examine them in the light of conscience. As he inherited and understood the concept, conscience was the practical faculty which mediated between universal law and particular

47

act. It involved assent to the universal rule (an act of the reason) and application to a particular case (an act of the will or judgement). 'And this is the nature of the equitable; correction of law where it is defective owing to its universality' (ARISTOTLE). Equity could be described as conscience in action in the field of practical or applied justice (M. FLEISHER, *RADICAL REFORM AND POLITICAL PERSUASION IN THE LIFE AND WRITINGS OF THOMAS MORE* 24).

Where Saint German tended to set out in detail the ways in which law could be evaluated in the light of conscience, More moved directly to equity – the will to act justly. True justice does not exist in the abstract, though a good lawyer must have thorough grasp of its principles. True justice lies in the application of just principles. This is practical justice, comparable to More's practical theology (which must be pastoral), or practical philosophy (which must be ethical or political). The common lawyer, like the canon lawyer, the theologian, or the philosopher 'must abandon the formal letter in order to uphold the human being' (FLEISHER 29). Even more importantly, equity reflects the way in which a just and merciful God deals with sinners. It embodies the 'new law of mercy', where God rules us 'as a father rules his children', not by the strict enforcement of law (U 22).

In *Utopia*, there were few laws, no lawyers, and no private property. In England, much of More's time was taken up settling disputes over property, and he tried to prevent the kind of continuous litigation which refused to take a court settlement as final. More's integrity and reputation as an 'incorruptible judge' were widely respected. William Daunce, his son-in-law, remarked that he did not gain financially from being related to More, as others related to those in high office seemed able to do. More congratulated him for his honesty, but ironically indicated there were more subtle ways open to the unscrupulous than accepting bribes: dropping a word or writing a letter in a friend's favour, hearing his case earlier, appointing a biased commission to hear his suit, returning a favour with another favour. More ended :

I assure you on my faith, that if the parties will at my hand call for justice, then ... were it my father stood on the one side and the devil on the other, his cause being good, the devil should have right.
(ROPER 220)

More and the Extermination of Heresy

In view of More's constant concern that the strict application of the law must be mitigated by mercy and equity, his vigorous campaign against the Protestant Reformers, whom he regarded as heretics, is difficult to understand. During Wolsey's time as chancellor, not a single person was put to death for his or her religious beliefs. During More's time of office (October 1529–May 1532), six men were burned at the stake as heretics, and More was personally involved in the detection of three of them. The accusations that More flogged heretics against a tree in his Chelsea garden, or stole property from them, must be discounted. More denied them and defended his integrity with great dignity in his *Apology* of 1533; there is no good reason to doubt his word. Yet the burning of heretics, the banning of heretical books, and the humiliating public penances for those found with them, were repressive measures which seem strangely at odds with More's earlier belief in religious toleration. The Utopians, we were told, held that 'no one should suffer on account of his religious beliefs' (U 97). Did More abandon his humanistic ideals because dangerous times required difficult decisions? Did he lay aside the radical vision of his younger days, to meet the demands of real politics? The answer is both difficult and complex.

More was proud of his campaign against heretics, and he mentions it in the epitaph he wrote to sum up his life, where he describes himself as 'grievous to thieves, murderers and heretics'. He wrote to Erasmus:

As to that statement in my epitaph that I was a source of trouble for heretics – I wrote that with deep feeling. I find that breed of men

*absolutely loathsome, so much so that, unless they regain their
senses, I want to be as hateful to them as anyone can possibly be;
for my increasing experience with those men frightens me with the
thought of what the world will suffer at their hands.* (SL 46)

One of the most damaging allegations made against More by revisionist biographers, such as Richard Marius, is that More 'cried out' for heretics to be burned. 'This fury was not a bizarre lapse in an otherwise noble character; it is almost the essence of the man' (R. MARIUS, *THOMAS MORE* XXIV). Though Marius exonerates More from personally torturing heretics in his house, such exaggerated rhetoric is not supported by the evidence. More viewed heresy much as a modern magistrate might view racism: as a repulsive and divisive civil and ecclesiastical danger (KENNY). He wanted a 'clean cutting out' of the infected part of the civic body, to ensure the survival of the rest. The evidence seems to point to More's having shouldered a grim responsibility, in the firm conviction that he was doing right, but not to any rejoicing or fanatical pleasure.

More's deepest reasons for prosecuting heretics were theological and religious: heresy was a kind of treason of the soul, and endangered the eternal salvation of other Christians. As More saw it, to put the soul of another person in jeopardy risked cutting that person off from God for all eternity. Such an action, he thought, deserved the death penalty, and with it the forlorn hope that it might produce a last-minute recantation.

By our standards the processes of the age were cruel and repellent. Nevertheless, More's fierce intolerance towards heretics, and the part he played in persecution, cannot be defended, and are at odds with his Utopian ideals. They are the negative side of his vision of a Christian society – a society united in religious allegiance and sharing a common life. The notion that a unified society depends on common values remains valid even today. In More's time this seemed to most people to exclude religious dissent. While we may understand his reasons, it remains deeply distressing that in this matter More was a man of his time, not a 'man for all seasons'.

Common Law, Canon Law and the King's Divorce

More and his legal contemporaries operated within two distinct systems of law, the common law of England and the canon law of the universal Church. More's immediate predecessors as chancellor had been canon lawyers. More was a common lawyer with a working knowledge of canon law. To More the common law represented the accumulated wisdom, grounded in human reason, of a temporal kingdom. Canon law represented the accumulated wisdom of spiritual authority, grounded in divine law or revelation. Kings as heads of their kingdoms, and the Pope as the visible head of the universal Church of Christ, held their power from God, and represented God to those they ruled. More believed he owed allegiance to each as part of the divine ordering of temporal and spiritual society.

Canon law, like common law, needed to be simplified and reformed. More naturally believed that the proper authority to do that was the Church, not the state. The failure of the Fifth Lateran Council of 1512–1517, a general council of the whole Church, to undertake the reform of canon law was a source of scandal which contributed to the Protestant Reformation. Many lawyers of the time thought that King and Parliament should intervene, especially if there was a conflict of jurisdiction. But More upheld the liberty and privileges of the Church, which must administer its own legal system. To do otherwise would subordinate the law of the universal Church to the law of one kingdom. So More, the modernizing reformer of the common law, was seen as the conservative defender of canon law.

Tension between the two systems of justice was very evident with regard to heresy trials. Two notorious cases occurred in the early years of Henry VIII's reign: those of Richard Hunne (1514) and Henry Standish (1517). Hunne was found hanged in his cell two days after his canon law trial for heresy. Then, as now, death while in custody aroused popular indignation; arguments for and against his possible suicide or judicial murder rumbled on for years. Standish was cited before a church court for arguing that a papal decree had no validity in England unless 'received' by Parliament. The King's discreet silence at the trial implied his agreement with Standish. The case was dropped.

Anti-clerical, or anti-papal, feeling was spasmodic rather than endemic in England, but could easily be aroused. There was a strong perception that English men and women should not be subject to 'foreign' laws, that many clerics were motivated by self-interest, not justice, and that canon law gave clerics an unfair privileged status. There were battles within the legal profession about the procedures adopted in the church courts. The Hunne case haunted popular imagination. More returned to it in five of his polemical works, each time defending the action of church authorities. His harsh policy against heretics was unpopular and fanned criticism of the Church.

An alleged heretic was brought to trial in a church court, and if found guilty and sentenced to death, was handed over to the secular authority for execution. This meant that someone accused of heresy was tried by one system and punished by another. Church courts used an *inquisitorial* system, where the judges sought to elicit the truth, sometimes requiring a suspect to take an oath of innocence or be tried as a heretic. Common law courts used an *adversarial* system, where the case for and against the accused was argued, and then judged by a jury. Both systems had advantages, and both were open to abuse. To most ordinary people the English jury system seemed preferable. From 1529 to 1532 More, as enforcer of the laws of heresy, had to defend them and canon law practice, and so was perceived as pro-clerical and traditionalist.

The issues of common law and canon law were to be focused most sharply in the matter of the King's request for an annulment of his marriage to Catherine of Aragon. Marriage questions were clearly within church jurisdiction. Not normally a patient man, Henry had suffered delays of three years (1526–1529), going through the usual ecclesiastical channels. He had no male heir, he had fallen in love with Anne Boleyn, and he thought he had grounds in canon law for declaring his first marriage illegal. When in June 1529 the ecclesiastical tribunal at Blackfriars declined to find in his favour, and referred the case to Rome, his anger knew no bounds. He was a sovereign king, used to getting his own way. Was he to appear as an ordinary plaintiff in a foreign court likely to find in his wife's favour?

Henry played the anti-clerical card to put pressure on the Pope. Wolsey had failed to get the King's divorce, so Wolsey had to be replaced. More, a layman, was appointed in his stead. Henry canvassed the opinions of European universities on the divorce question, and anxiously awaited the outcome. However, from late 1530 onwards new and more radical ideas began to spread. Could a king of England be lawfully summoned to a court outside his realm? Was not the King both Emperor (temporal leader) and Pope (spiritual leader) within that realm? Could he not empower Parliament to grant the divorce, irrespective of papal permission? These ideas were as yet tentative but were to gain ground steadily, especially among the supporters of Anne Boleyn, who brought them to Henry's attention. Above all they were very ably presented by an anonymous writer, who we now know to have been the brilliant lawyer, Christopher Saint German. Impeccably orthodox in his doctrinal beliefs, he was to become More's polemical and political opponent, because he denied the long-standing tradition of the legal and juridical independence of the Church.

The slow and tentative emergence of the concept of the royal (rather then papal) supremacy of the Church in England was clearly bound up with Henry's need for a divorce. It coincided with the ideals of emerging Protestant thinkers who had religious grounds for breaking with Rome, and of common lawyers who disliked the dual systems of justice. This More saw very clearly, but there was very little he could do. Once again he found himself defending the religious and constitutional *status quo.*

Henry had to find a way to put pressure on the English clergy to support his case. By February 1531 the clergy had been charged under an old statute for having exercised their spiritual jurisdiction directly from the Pope, bypassing the King. They begged pardon, paid a fine and acknowledged Henry as Supreme Head of the Church in England, 'as far as the law of Christ allows'. A year later, on 15 May 1532, the Convocation of the Clergy (except for John Fisher, Bishop of Rochester) submitted to Henry's authority as Supreme Head, without a proviso. The following day More handed his seal of office back to Henry on grounds of 'not being equal to the work'. More agreed with Fisher that 'the fort had been betrayed even by them that should have defended it'. He later declared that the King had been allowed to get his own way because of a 'flexible Council ... and a weak clergy', who had failed in their duty to give him the advice he had not wanted to hear. Since More could not prevent the divorce, nor the religious and constitutional changes needed to provide it, he had no alternative but to resign.

More's resignation from public office and public life was not only an admission of political defeat; it marked the end of his trial of 'practical philosophy', and his desire not to abandon the ship of state when it ran into a storm. The moral and the expedient were clearly incompatible. He could not be part of a government which declared that a lay ruler had spiritual jurisdiction over the Church of Christ – even that part which was his realm. As More saw it, what Henry proposed to do was to cut a living branch off the tree that was a united Christendom. At his trial More expressed his position clearly:

This realm, being but one member and small part of the church,
might not make a particular law disagreeable with the general law

of the Christ's universal church catholic, no more than the city of London, being but one poor member in respect of the whole realm, might make a law against an act of Parliament to bind the whole realm. (ROPER 248)

Henry and Anne Boleyn were secretly married in January 1533. Henry was granted an annulment in an English church court by Cranmer, now Archbishop of Canterbury, and on Whit Sunday 1533 Anne was crowned Queen of England. More, living in impoverished retirement at Chelsea, refused to attend her coronation, even though Tunstall and others had begged him to do so. In his reply to them, he cited an old story about an emperor bound by a law which prevented him from carrying out a death sentence on a virgin. It did not take long to find a way around the law 'by first deflowering her and then devouring her'. More pointed out that by attending Anne Boleyn's coronation, the bishops were compromising their integrity. 'Now my Lords it lieth not in my power but that they may devour me. But God, being my good Lord, I will provide that they shall never deflower me' (ROPER 230). More's imprisonment was only a matter of time.

In retirement, More had only one weapon left: to continue to write in defence of the faith of Christendom. The next chapter will consider More as a polemical writer, a role he assumed from 1523 onwards when he first wrote against Luther.

5

In Defence of Christendom
Polemical Writings 1523–1533

To insult anyone does not demand any skill; it is neither a gentle-manly thing to do, nor the mark of a good man.   (MORE TO DORP 1515)

The writer of polemic is of necessity ungenerous and unfair. (LOUIS MARTZ)

In the same year in which Thomas More entered the King's service (1517), Martin Luther published his famous theses against indulgences at the University of Wittenberg. By 1521 he had been summoned before the Emperor Charles V at the German Assembly, or Diet of Worms. He refused to recant, declaring 'Here I stand and can do none other'. But for the protection of his prince, Luther would almost certainly have been handed over to the secular arm and burned as a heretic. Martin Luther and Thomas More were each to make a famous stand on conscience, in the consciousness that before God they could not act otherwise. This they were to do from different sides of the religious divide.

Luther's excommunication from the universal Church took effect from 1521; his most famous Reformation writings date from the previous year, and their contents had spread rapidly. His treatise *To The Christian Nobility of the German Nation* called on the German Princes to remember their priestly vocation, given at baptism, and to act decisively to reform the Church. *The Babylonian Captivity of the Church* was an attack on the authority of the

papacy and on Catholic teaching concerning the seven sacraments. On 21 May 1521 Luther's books were publicly burned at St
Paul's Cross in London – a symbolic act affirming England's loyalty to the papacy and to orthodoxy. Henry VIII wanted to make his
contribution to the rebuttal of heresy; he wrote (with help) his
Assertion of the Seven Sacraments against Luther's rejection of five
of the seven. Henry took such a high view of papal authority that
More cautioned him, suggesting he amended the text and 'more
slenderly touched' papal power (ROPER 235).

Luther replied to Henry in an unpleasant and vituperative pam-
phlet to which a king could not respond without loss of dignity. A
substantive theological answer to Luther had already been written by Bishop John Fisher. More was allocated the task of demolishing the enemy in a more popular and accessible way. He did so
(using a pseudonym) in his *Responsio ad Lutherum* (1523) and in
language hardly less restrained than Luther's. Though at first
reluctant, he was soon drawn so passionately into the controversy
that he produced a second and expanded edition. Luther's attack
on the institutional church had touched a topic central to More's
beliefs and religious commitment: the nature and identity of the
Christian Church. It was More's first major work of popular religious polemic, written in Latin for a continental audience, and
part of a sustained official programme to discredit Lutheranism.

Theological Method: The Nature of Polemic

As a young humanist More had been intensely critical of the older,
scholastic theology of the late Middle Ages, because it was combative, proffering the 'clenched fist' rather than the 'outstretched
palm' of friendship. His preferred mode of theology was the dialogue, or conversation among friends at table or in a garden,
where shared insight stimulated discussion. But what happens
when there is no dialogue and no sharing of minds? The tolerance
of the 'good pagans' in *Utopia* was based on the presumption that

when Christianity was preached to them they would come to accept it. By 1523 More was aware that what he and Erasmus had written as reforming humanists before 1517 could be taken out of context in later, more difficult times. He would rather burn his books, or those of his friend, than cause scandal or misunderstanding.

Humanist theology broke down when friendly discussion failed to convince or persuade. Ironically it then had to revert to the adversarial style, and the polemical method of rebutting arguments, used by medieval theologians. It was generally accepted, by all sides, that error had no rights, and that to persist in error indicated either wilful blindness or great stupidity. The appropriate response to heresy was to root it out, since dissent from truth was potentially subversive. Polemical theologians tried to discredit not just the beliefs but the motivation and integrity of the enemy; almost any verbal tactic was admissible. As has already been said, a humanist was well equipped to make this shift from the dialogical to the polemical method, for he was not simply a man of peace but one trained in the art of using language appropriate to the occasion (MARTZ 21).

Many humanists found it hard to adapt their rhetoric of persuasion to the demands of controversy. The need to defeat became more urgent than the desire to persuade; the defence of doctrine more urgent than the pastoral needs of the individual. More, far more than Erasmus, found himself abandoning his humanistic programme for the duration of the Reformation emergency. In his polemical writings, More's attitude 'is not that of a judge standing above the contest and weighing carefully both pleadings. It is rather that of a barrister or advocate who has taken the position that the defendant is guilty' (HEADLY, INTRODUCTION TO CW5 813). In 1523, when More took on Luther, he had not had an opportunity to read very much of his opponent's writings. He relied on hearsay and rumour, and was probably influenced by contact with Thomas Murner, a German Franciscan, then in England and at court.

More Versus Luther (1523)

In the more open and tolerant climate of today we find the violence and intolerance of Reformation polemic very hard to understand. More's language is often immoderate, unfair and even scurrilous. In the *Responsio* More portrayed Luther as 'Luder', the buffoon (Latin, *ludere*, to play), or as Lewder, the shameful.

> *Men will recall and say that once long ago there was in a former age a certain rascal by the name of Luther who ... in order to adorn his sect with fitting emblems, surpassed magpies in chatter, pimps in wickedness, prostitutes in obscenity, all buffoons in buffoonery.*
> (CW5 684)

But beneath the unpleasant polemic, More began to shape his own contribution to ecclesiology (discussion on the nature of the Church) in answer to Luther's attack on the visible, institutional Church. More believed in a Church which he identified with the common, known, visible multitude of believers, spread throughout the world and down the ages. This visible community was the bearer and interpreter of revelation, of what God had revealed to us in Jesus Christ:

> *The common, known, Catholic people, clergy, lay folk and all, which whatever their language be ... do stand together and agree in confession of the one true Catholic faith.* (CW5 1 139)

More saw this living tradition as enduring in the Church. The Church is a living community, embodied in time and space. His preferred description of this was the *common corps of Christendom*. In the Middle Ages the concept of Christendom had developed as the Christian equivalent of Islam, and was primarily a religious concept; but for all practical purposes it was geographically located in Europe, and transcended national boundaries and interests.

Under the spiritual leadership of the Pope, it became a visible expression of the unity of Christian faith and practice, in a culture which equated baptism with full citizenship. The enemies of Christendom were the *infidel* (outside the corporate body) and the *heretic* (within the corporate body). The infidel was most usually seen as the Ottoman Turk.

More saw the Church as a common (or ordinary) Church of saints and sinners. More's belief in the *consensus* (or *common sense*) of faith and practice, was somewhat similar to his belief, as a lawyer, in the *consensus* of the people of England embodied in the common law of the land. More remained in touch with the ordinary folk who thronged into his courts seeking justice. These people made up the *City of God* on earth. Jesus Christ had given this living community of faith the gift of the presence of the Holy Spirit. The Spirit was the guarantor of its fidelity to its origins, despite the clear evidence of the sinfulness of many of its members, including some of its leaders.

This Spirit of God was present not only in the *collective* consciousness of the community, but in the *individual* consciousness of each baptized Christian. More, like Luther, believed in the gospel written by God in the hearts of all Christians. But he stressed the reciprocity between the community of faith guided by the Spirit, and the individual inner response to that same Spirit. 'The inner gospel [of the heart] was for More, at least at this time, the primary means by which divine revelation was transmitted from generation to generation within the believing community' (GOGAN 92–3).

> On the heart, therefore, in the Church of Christ, there remains the true gospel of Christ which was written there before the books of all the evangelists. (CW5 1 100) *The gospel is written with the greatest certainty in the hearts of men.* (MARGINAL GLOSS TO RESPONSIO)

More could not accept Luther's rejection of the living tradition of the Church, in order to return to the 'pure word' of Scripture. He constantly paraphrased Augustine's dictum that 'he would not have believed the gospel were it not for the authority of the Church'. The gospel has come down to us in and through tradition. It was written in the hearts of those who received the good news, before it was written down in a book. For More, Luther's stress on the written, necessarily external word, was a return to the old law, and a movement away from the gospel of the new covenant:

> Is not Luther moved at all by the words of God, mentioned also by the Apostles: 'I will put my laws upon their hearts and upon their minds I will write them'? He wrote the old law first on stone, later on wood, yet always externally. He will write the new law inwardly by the finger of God on the book of the heart ... what he has written on the heart will last indelibly. (CW5 1 100)

In the warmer ecumenical climate of today, we can see more clearly what divided More and Luther, two great Christians. More never had any insight into, or understanding of, what made Luther reject the institutional Church. Luther's experience of the human face of the Church had led him to doubt whether it could be a vehicle for divine revelation. He came to see the papacy and the papal administration as something which had developed during the history of Christianity, with no sure foundation in Scripture. The papacy, its legalistic canon law, and the burdens it had laid on the Christian conscience, had obscured rather than mediated the Christian gospel. Luther considered that if he could 'get behind' the barnacles of accumulated tradition, and reclaim the simple message of the gospel, he could hear the true word of God. This word would touch the heart and change the direction of Christian life. It followed that the 'true Church' consisted of those who heard the word of God here and now, and kept it by God's gift of faith.

Luther's Church was an invisible Church of the 'elect', known only to God.

More attacked Luther's 'Church of the Elect', which was utterly different from his 'Church of all common folk'. More could be *sure* that the Church was the bearer of Christ's teaching because of its organic continuity from apostolic times to the present. Luther could only be *sure*, if the word was preached and heard here and now, in a community ready to accept it. An unreformed, 'ungodly', community was unable to 'hear' the Word of God. Both men sought *certitude*. There was little room for compromise since these were truths necessary for salvation. More strongly opposed Luther's attempt to define the true Church according to its invisible, interior and purely spiritual nature.

More's attitude to the papacy needs special attention. He never held a high authoritarian view of the pope, though his later stand against Henry VIII invited this interpretation. He naturally inclined towards papal primacy, rather than the papal sovereignty. Only Christ the Lord held 'sovereignty' over human persons. The pope was Christ's visible representative on earth. More insisted that he would ever have brought up the question of papal authority if Luther had not entangled it with the nature of the Church, and so forced him to do so (CW5 1 139). After the Council of Trent (1545), post-reformation Catholicism naturally turned to popes and General Councils for guidance in matters of faith. The touchstone for More was not so much teaching authority 'from above' as the universal faith of the Christian community, spread through space and time. More was the heir of the theology of the early Church Fathers, who appealed to 'what has been believed everywhere, always, and by all' (RULE OF VINCENT OF LERINS). This was the criterion of orthodoxy which it was the duty of leadership to preserve and uphold. This was the essence of what it meant to be *Catholic* or *universal*. It was for this *Catholicism*, (under papal primacy) that More was eventually to die.

Luther's distinction between law and gospel, and his exaltation of gospel and condemnation of law, presented particular difficulties for More. As a lawyer, More valued the function of common law as a guarantor of liberty, and the exercise of equity where it might fail to do so. Luther claimed that the justified man needed neither the guidance nor the restriction of the law 'but accompanies the law through a love which is rooted in faith'. Luther tended to agree with Plato (*Politics*) that the rule of a gifted magistrate might be preferable to a body of laws. To More, the common lawyer, this was sheer madness. He regarded Luther's treatise on *The Freedom of the Christian* as a recipe for anarchy, and feared its socio-political consequences. His worst fears seemed to have been realized when the so-called Peasants' Revolt broke out in Germany (1524–1525). Later More was to blame the horrendous sack of Rome (1527) on Luther's rabble-rousing language. (In fact Rome was sacked by the mercenaries of the Catholic Emperor Charles V.) Luther feared social anarchy as much as More did. But Luther's rhetoric of Christian freedom forced More into giving a greater emphasis to the role of all authority, including papal authority.

More had a special dislike of those who 'broke their word'; in a civilized society a man's word was his bond. He constantly returned to the theme of perjury as a breach of faith, a misuse of the common language of trust, or the breaking of a solemn undertaking. He wrote a memorandum on the topic while in the Tower. One form of perjury he particularly disliked: the breaking of religious vows (CW5 11 763–9). His most strongly worded invective against Luther concerned his marriage, for Luther had been a friar who abandoned his vows. One of the reasons More denounced heretics was that they had deliberately 'broken faith' with their baptismal promises.

More was intent on demolishing Luther's arguments: he gave less attention to the systematic exposition of his own. However, these were the early years of formulating a Catholic response to the Reformers. More developed his ideas further is his *Letter to Bugenhagen* (1526), friend of Luther and pastor in Wittenberg. In these Lutheran controversies he first forged his great themes on the nature of the Church: the common corps of Christendom, the common sense of the faith held by all Christians, the guidance of the Spirit, the gospel written in the hearts of the faithful, the law which is not opposed to the freedom of the gospel, the papacy as embodying Christian unity. However, from 1526 onwards More's most urgent task was to confront English rather than continental reformers.

More Versus William Tyndale (1526–1533)

By 1526 the work of English evangelical Reformers was taking firmer shape and influencing a wider circle of English men and women. The bitter exchanges between Thomas More and William Tyndale, two gifted Englishmen, were a tragedy. Tyndale, a brilliant linguist and translator of the Bible, was exiled from England, settled in Germany and became deeply influenced by Luther. In 1526 his pocket-sized translations of the New Testament in English were smuggled into the country, and ruthlessly hunted down by church and state authorities. But in spite of this, many of Tyndale's apt and memorable phrases passed into the English of the Authorized Version (1611) and so into our common Christian understanding: 'Let there be light', 'we live and move and have our being', 'fight the good fight', 'the salt of the earth', and many more. The words of the familiar English biblical stories of creation or the teaching of Jesus are usually Tyndale's. This was the best possible vindication of the humanist desire to make the Bible available to the 'ploughman at his plough', and in his own language. More did not object to the Latin translation of the New Testament which Erasmus published in 1516. So why did he so bitterly attack Tyndale's English translation some ten years later?

Tyndale's translation was part of the Reformer's rejection of tradition in favour of a return to 'pure' Scriptures. Tyndale's key words and annotations were theological choices, favouring a

Reforming, evangelical interpretation of Christian life and practice. More took issue with Tyndale over his substitution of new, for well known, translations of six key ecclesiastical terms: 'love' for 'charity', 'congregation' for 'church', 'senior or elder' for 'priest', 'favour' for 'grace', 'repentance' for 'do penance'. More was less interested in the exact origin of a biblical word than in its common usage and understanding. As More saw it, Tyndale was not a humanist making the Scriptures available in the vernacular, but a Reformer tilting his translations in support of his new beliefs.

Tyndale followed the success of his translation of the New Testament with *The Parable of the Wicked Mammon*, on justification by faith alone, and *The Obedience of a Christian Man*, on princely sovereignty. These were worrying developments. So in 1528 Tunstall, Bishop of London, officially commissioned More to read prohibited books and to defend the Catholic position. More's *A Dialogue Concerning Heresies* was first published in 1529 and revised in 1531, when he was Chancellor. It is written in English and is usually considered the best of his polemical works.

Like Utopia, *A Dialogue Concerning Heresies* was cast in the form of a fictitious conversation. A friend of More's supposedly sends his children's tutor as a 'Messenger' or go-between, to discuss with More disturbing aspects of popular religious opinion. The Messenger is himself attracted to some of these new reforming ideas and is 'confused'. He senses (possibly shares) the strong public distaste for the hunting down of heretics, and the mood of anti-clericalism. In this book More intends to address the 'common citizen' of London, capital of the book trade and a main source for obtaining heretical books from abroad. The *Dialogue* is filled with references to events known to Londoners, such as the case of Richard Hunne, and to places like St Paul's Cross, where heretical books were burned. There, in 1526, Thomas Bilney and the fire steelyard merchants had been forced to abjure and to carry faggots to the great bonfire. The opinion of Londoners was a crucial factor in the war of religious and political propaganda. The Messenger, a 'representative Londoner', is drawn into the domestic space of More's home and subjected to his 'gentle' art of advocacy (CW6 INTRODUCTION).

The *Dialogue* has many of More's best merry tales, proverbs and witticisms, and is clearly a work for popular consumption. More and his questioner would have had *The Canterbury Tales* in mind as they discussed the merits of going on pilgrimage. The *Dialogue* deals with the criticisms directed by the Reformers at popular piety: the cult of saints, belief in miracles, use of relics, images, pilgrimages. It tackled criticism of a supposedly corrupt and ill-educated clergy. Central to all these arguments was the question of the nature of the Church.

More expounded his conviction of the abiding presence of Christ and his Spirit in the living community of the Church from generation to generation. This living tradition includes beliefs and also customs, and every aspect of the corporate life of the Church (GOGAN 143). It included

> all the devout rites and ceremonies of the church, both in the divine service as incensing, hallowing of the fire, of the font, of the paschal lamb, and over all that the exorcisms, benedictions and holy strange gestures used in consecration or ministration of the blessed sacrament, all which holy things great part whereof was from hand to mouth left in the church, from the time of Christ's apostles and by them left to us.   (CW6 55-6)

More was well aware that not all custom dated from the early Church, and that change was part of natural growth. But he had an instinctive respect for the social and religious power of customs and rites, both to bond a community and to transmit the faith. His was a strongly sacramental view of the world: human beings needed the tangible and the material through which the spiritual could be disclosed. He was aware of the shift from the medieval visual culture to the new 'book culture' of the printed word. But what are words but verbal images, and what are names but images of personal identity? (CW6 46) Traditionally, visual images were the layman's book for those who could not read. Elsewhere More argued that *all* Christians, whether literate or not, needed visual images. He would have agreed with a modern definition of human beings as image, or symbol, makers.

> For as I somewhat said unto you before, all the words that be either written or spoken, be but images representing the things that the writer or speaker conceiveth in the mind; likewise as the figure of the thing framed with imagination and so conceived in the mind, is but an image representing the very thing itself that a man thinketh on. (CW6 46)

Recent research has revealed once more the desolation experienced in many English parishes when uncomprehending parishioners were stripped of their religious customs and popular forms of piety during the English Reformations (CF. EAMON DUFFY, *THE STRIPPING OF THE ALTARS: TRADITIONAL RELIGION IN ENGLAND 1400–1500*, 1992). This is not to underestimate the criticisms of those who saw the lush abundance and uncritical piety of some late medieval devotion as quasi-magical, and superstitious. But the reform of custom and rite is not the same as its abolition, and contemporary social anthropologists are much more wary of dismissing popular piety as 'mere superstition'. More's defence of many aspects of popular practice should not be seen as just traditionalist, hard-line and predictably anti-Reformer. He regarded all customs as part of the warp and woof of society. If here and there threads were pulled out, the whole was unravelled and spoiled.

Another of More's concerns in these controversies was Tyndale's conviction that the souls of the dead remained asleep in the 'bosom of Abraham' until the day of resurrection. Luther had proposed this far more cautiously. Such a belief did away with the Catholic doctrine of purgatory, or belief in a place of purification for souls after death and before admission to heaven. If the souls of the dead were not conscious they could not be helped. Equally the saints could not help the Church on earth because they too were in 'soul-sleep'.

The point here is not to rehearse arguments which divided Catholic and Protestant thought, or which may not interest a modern reader. But for late-medieval people the concept of 'kith and kin' extended beyond the grave. Saints were friends who could intercede in heaven for family and friends on earth. Religious confraternities, and chantries or chapels where mass was said for the dead, expressed a continued bondedness with an extended family, which had passed from this life to the next. The belief in the Church as a Communion of Saints, on earth, in heaven, and in purgatory, was part of common ecclesial understanding. To deny the existence of purgatory, or the cult of the saints, demolished what Berger has called the 'sacred canopy', which gave people their bearings and their world-view. More was convinced that this was destructive and dangerous to both religion and society, and had no warrant in tradition. The Reformers felt such practices had no warrant in Scripture.

More took issue with Tyndale over his belief in justification by faith alone, which seemed to More to deny a role to 'good works'. Luther and Tyndale were reacting against what they saw as self-reliance rather than God-reliance in Christian faith and practice. Their Reformation insight was the joy of discovering that faith and justification were God's pure gift, not something merited by human effort. In doing so they denied a role to the human will and to co-operation with God's grace in the process of human redemption. This ran counter to humanist belief in the power of human beings to shape their own destiny, and to be co-workers with God in creating a civilized world and society. To live life was a 'work' given us by a creator God, who would always give the grace to cope with any circumstance. More dismissed Tyndale's 'feeling faith' as subjective and morally dangerous: how could human beings *not* work out their salvation with the help of God's grace? In life, and in his crisis in the Tower, he had a strong sense of God 'ever at his elbow', enabling and strengthening his purpose. There were to be misunderstandings on both sides in discussion on this burning issue.

Tyndale replied to More's *Dialogue Concerning Heresies* in a treatise of about ninety thousand words, published in Antwerp in 1530. More replied in a massive work of controversy: *The Confutation of Tyndale's Answer*, in nine books and half a million words. To the modern reader such length is tedious beyond belief. Yet these books, and especially the *Dialogue*, contain important ideas. There is no doubt but that the pressure of political events and his resignation affected the quality and sharpness of More's writing. But he still managed to produce passages of brilliant wit and persuasive power, and to use digression as a strategy to bring the wandering mind back to the heart of the argument. More's mind had not disintegrated (as some critics have suggested), but his world was in the process of so doing, and the strain showed.

In Defence of The Doctrine of The Eucharist (1533–1534)

During the last months before his imprisonment (autumn 1533 to April 1534), More wrote four books in defence of the doctrine of the eucharist. It is possible that the last two were completed in prison; they were unpublished in his lifetime. Why was the doctrine of the eucharist so central to More during these last months of freedom? More, like Fisher, did not regard the eucharist primarily in devotional or individualistic terms but as *constitutive* of the unity of the Church. The primary sense of the 'real presence' of Christ was his whole body, the Church. The 'real presence' of Jesus in the eucharist allowed Christians to enter into this truth more fully. It was the sacramental celebration of what God had done for us in Jesus Christ. Political opposition to royal supremacy, and theological opposition to the English Reformers who denied the doctrine of a *real* presence, were two distinct but related ways of confronting those who sought to break up the unity of Christendom.

In October 1532, John Frith, an associate of Tyndale, was imprisoned in the Tower, and wrote there a short treatise on the eucharist. A copy came into More's hands and he prepared a reply. In April 1533 an anonymous tract, *The Souper of the Lord*, appeared, defending Frith's approach to the eucharist, that is as a meal of remembrance. (Either Tyndale or George Joye was the anonymous author.) After Frith was burned at Smithfield on 4 July 1533, the debate became a major political issue. During the autumn of 1533 More prepared part one of his *Answer to a Poisoned Book* which he published in December, together with his *Letter to John Frith*.

Dubbed 'Master Mock' by his unknown opponent, More in his *Answer* named him 'Master Masker', ridiculing one who hid behind the mask of anonymity, although More had done this himself against Luther. The theme of 'masks and realities' was brilliantly exploited by More, both linguistically and theologically. A mask *hides* the reality of the human person; the eucharistic sign *discloses* the mysterious reality of the Christian's incorporation into Christ, and the 'loving connectedness of all things' in God's providential plan for humankind. Belief in a *real* and not merely *signified* presence was crucial for More's understanding of the gathering together of the many into the one body of Christ, both on earth and in heaven. More did not rely on scholastic arguments: the medieval word 'transubstantiation', meaning the change of the substances of bread and wine into the body and blood of Christ, was never mentioned. More used scriptural and early church sources to support his thesis. When he returned to these sources he used the latest translations and critical editions of the texts. Here was More, the humanist, retrieving the ancient tradition by the most modern scholarship.

More's last eucharistic writings have come to us under the titles *A Treatise on the Passion* and *A Treatise to Receive the Blessed Body of*

Our Lord. Together they may have been intended to be the second part of his *Answer to a Poisoned Book.* Whether or not they were partly composed in the Tower, they belong to the devotional and (almost) non-controversial discourse that characterized More's Tower writings. Between December 1533 and his imprisonment on 17 April 1534, More had personal reasons for linking his own situation with the eucharist, Christ's gift to his disciples on the night before he suffered. More wrote that henceforth all his energies would be focused on the passion and death of Jesus Christ, and on his own passage from this world. In the end More, like Tyndale, turned to the comfort and consolation of the scriptural word of God, as he prepared the defence of his conscience.

Facing Defeat

By early 1534 More was exhausted. As a statesman and writer he had failed to stem the tide of change. Once Roper had congratulated him on his success against heretics. More had replied enigmatically:

> *And yet, son Roper, I pray God that some of us, as high as we seem to sit upon the mountains treading heretics under our feet like ants, live not in the day that we would gladly wish to be at league and composition with them to let them have their churches quietly to themselves, so that they would be content to let us have ours quietly to ourselves.* (ROPER 216)

More did not want mutual tolerance, a day when Christians of differing persuasions would agree to live and let live, because it would mean acknowledging the breakup of Christendom, which he held to be most precious. But the breakup of Christendom into the new nation states, each with their own state church, was at hand. And, unbelievably, there would come a day when a future pope, John Paul II, would declare Luther to be 'a man of faith' for all Christians (1983). A new kind of Christian unity would be painfully forged from the collapse of the old.

Both More and Tyndale were to die for their religious beliefs. Tyndale's imprisonment in Vilvoorde, outside Brussels, was to overlap with that of More, and he was to be strangled, then burned as a heretic, just one year after More's execution as a traitor.

6

In Defence of Conscience
Tower Writings 1534–1535

I die the King's good servant, but God's first.   (MORE BEFORE HIS
EXECUTION)

In May 1533, when Archbishop Cranmer pronounced the marriage of Henry VIII and Catherine of Aragon null and void, More remarked to Roper: 'God give me grace, good son, that these matters within a while, be not confirmed with oath.' On 12 April 1534, More was summoned to Lambeth Palace to swear an oath of allegiance to the new Act of Succession, which proclaimed Anne as rightful Queen, and the issue of the second marriage as rightful heirs. On Monday, 13 April 1534, More attended mass at his parish church in Chelsea, said goodbye to his family at the gate to his garden, and took his barge downstream to Lambeth. After some time in silence, More turned to Roper and whispered: 'Son Roper, I thank God the field is won.' Roper only understood later that More did not expect to come home again, and that parting from his family was the hardest part of his long battle.

At Lambeth, More was the first, and the only layman to have the oath tendered to him by Archbishop Cranmer, and Cromwell, the King's secretary. More read the documents carefully and found himself able to swear to the Act of Succession itself, since the King in Parliament had the absolute right to determine who should succeed to the throne. But in conscience he could not subscribe to the preamble to the Act, which implied royal headship of the Church in England. He also refused to give his reasons for refusal. He was sent away to think things over, and from an upper room saw many of his clerical friends come and go, having no qualms about taking the oath. The only other person to refuse was John Fisher, Bishop of Rochester. More wrote a full account of his interrogation to his daughter, Margaret, a few days later:

> But as for myself in good faith my conscience so moved me in the matter that though I would not deny to swear to the succession, yet unto the oath that there was offered me I could not swear without the jeoparding of my soul to perpetual damnation. (SL 54 219)

More was called back for further questioning. The commissioners argued that this was a matter where More was bound to obey his sovereign Lord and King. More replied that

> this was one of the cases in which I was bounden that I should not obey my prince, sith that whatsoever other folk thought in the matter (whose conscience and learning I would not condemn nor take upon me to judge) yet in my conscience the truth seemed on the other side. Wherein I had not informed my conscience neither suddenly nor slightly but by long leisure and diligent search for the matter (SL 54 221)

It was pointed out to More that he had cause to fear setting his own opinion against the Parliament of the whole realm. More appealed to a wider General Council of the whole Church: 'I am not bounden to change my conscience and confirm it to the council of one realm, against the council of Christendom.' As for the oath:

> I never withdrew any man from it, nor never advised any to refuse it, nor never put, nor will, any scruple in any man's head, but leave every man to his own conscience. And methinketh in good faith, that so were it good reason that every man should leave me to mine. (SL 54 222)

More was given four days to reconsider his position. Refusing the oath yet again, he was sent to the Tower of London on 17 April 1534. For the next fifteen months More continued to refuse the oath, and to maintain official public silence about his reasons for refusal. Yet all his prison writings and recorded conversations were related indirectly to the defence of his conscience, as he tried to explain to family and friends why he had to make this stand. He had to do so in a way which was discreet, so that nothing he said or wrote could be construed against him in court. In the privacy of his prayer and personal meditation, he had to continue to discern whether he was taking the right action or not. This *outer* dialogue, with friends, and *inner* dialogue, with God and his conscience, pursued within a strategy of legal prudence and hardheadedness, constituted the core of his prison experience. His prison writings in defence of conscience, and in preparation for death, are among the finest in the whole Christian tradition.

Conscience and Consciousness

The role of conscience in the imprisonment and trial of Thomas More assumed an importance in sixteenth-century religious history only comparable to that of Martin Luther (1521). On that occasion Luther had said:

> *Unless I am convinced by the testimony of the scriptures or by clear reason, I am bound by the Scriptures I have quoted and my conscience is captive to the Word of God. I cannot and I will not retract anything, since it is neither safe nor right to go against conscience.* (LW 40 201)

For Luther and for More, conscience was not formed from a sense of the human rights of an individual person, but from a sense of the inner being of each human person as open to the scrutiny of God. For Luther, the freedom of the Christian conscience lay in being 'captive to the Word of God' addressed to the human heart. For More, the ultimate dignity of all human persons lay in the capacity of the 'eye of the heart' to see and act upon God's will. For both, God's ultimate and final judgement was all that mattered. Conscience was not self-determined, as in our contemporary understanding, but determined between the self and God. Peace, assurance and certainty of conscience lay in the grace of God towards human beings, for God alone is true and reliable, especially when all else fails.

In the sixteenth century the word *conscience* (derived from the Latin *scientia*, knowledge) stood not only for *inner*, moral self-awareness, but also for *outer* consciousness of the self in relation to the world and reality. There was no separate word for this outer consciousness; conscience stood for both inner and outer awareness; integrity was precisely the integration of both. If a person spoke, acted or wrote something which was not consistent with inner conviction, he or she lacked integrity and acted in bad conscience. In their different situations both More and Luther were asked to subscribe to something at variance with inner conviction. On trial and under oath, they were being asked to call upon God to attest to the truth of what they were saying, that is to perjure themselves. In More's case, a former judge was being asked both to perjure himself and to betray his profession.

More's prison writings constitute one of the most moving accounts of a Christian conscience striving to act morally and truthfully in a difficult situation. For More, conscience was firstly an activity of the intellect: the power to judge the past (what has been done), the future (what should be done), and the present (the reliability of one's convictions). But it was also an activity of the will: the power not only to judge but to act. As such the will was subject to many searing emotions: fear, anger, resentment, tedium, love of family, suicidal despair. More understood that these emotions had to be recognized and dealt with. But worst of all there was the experience of one's whole familiar world falling apart, and life itself threatened. How does conscience operate then? What are its compass bearings? How can one be sure of anything, or what comfort can be offered then?

The 'Little' Dialogue of Comfort: More and Margaret

The most poignant defence of More's conscience appears in the thirteen prison letters which survive – eight written to his daughter, Margaret, and five to friends. The longest and most significant was a further one supposedly written by Margaret to her step-sister Alice Alington, but in all probability composed by Margaret and More together. Alice had accidentally met the new chancellor, Lord Audley, and tried to plead More's cause. By means of a friendly warning, conveyed in two fables of Aesop about foolishness, Audley told More, via Alice, that by differing from the commonly held opinion of his peers, he appeared to most to be an obstinate fool. The Council considered More's refusal of the oath to be a foolish scruple over a mere trifle. Put succinctly, Audley's coded message to More was: try to find a way to trim your conscience to political reality, and save us all embarrassment.

Alice wrote to Margaret, who brought her letter to More in prison. Together they argued the case and composed an answer in which the word conscience appeared more than forty times. More and Erasmus had often enjoyed the use of a pun on More's name, which in Greek was close to *Moria* or folly. Erasmus' *In Praise of Folly* (1509) was written in praise of that Christian foolishness which turned out to be wisdom, but also in praise of his wise friend Thomas More, who so enjoyed playing the fool. More remembered this as he read the letter and weighed his arguments carefully, and it provided him with a line of defence.

If Audley conveyed his message by way of two parables about fools, More replied in kind. His was a story about an honest but slow-witted juryman who refused to perjure himself with the majority. In a court of law, even a fool was entitled to his conscience; and in a court of law, as the Council well knew, More was no fool. More tried to put Margaret at ease by laughing off foolish public opinion, before getting down to the serious part of his argument. A matter of conscience is no trifle, no mere scruple, no wisp of straw, but the very heart of what it is to be human.

More and Margaret discussed how he had arrived at his decision, of how dissent from a majority opinion might be, but also need not be, the mark of a misguided, foolish or obstinate mind. But for all More's awareness of the communal and communitarian aspects of human and Christian living, he believed that in the matter of conscience each human person was answerable to God alone. At the final judgement no one can take another's place or accept responsibility for another's conscience. 'And since I look in this matter only to God, it matters little to me that men ... say it is no conscience but only a foolish scruple.' In coming to his decision he had not even been influenced by his distinguished fellow prisoner John Fisher, one of the most learned in the land.

> Verily, daughter, I never intend (God being my good lord) to pin my soul on another man's back, not even the best man I know this day living; for I know not whither he may happen to carry it. There is no man living, of whom while he liveth, I may make myself sure ... If mine own conscience allowed me [to take the oath] I would not fail to do it though other men refuse, so though others refuse not, I dare not do it, mine own conscience standing against it. (ROGERS 206)

As for the law of the land, though each citizen is required to obey it, 'yet there is no man bound to swear that every law is well made'. Laws can be changed, improved, reformed, or revised. New laws can be brought in which some may think good, and others bad. But those who disapprove cannot be made to act against conscience. More would only allow one case where the individual should strive to conform conscience to a broader majority decision: that of a decision passed by a lawfully assembled General Council of the whole of Christendom. To dissent from such a law should be an occasion to 'move him, yet not compel him to conform his mind and conscience unto theirs'. More concluded:

> This is like a riddle, a case in which a man may lose his head and have no harm ... And therefore, mine own good daughter, never trouble your mind for anything that shall ever happen to me in this world. Nothing can come but that which God wills. And I am very sure that whatsoever that may be, however bad it may appear, it shall indeed be the best. (ROGERS 206)

A Dialogue of Comfort Against Tribulation

In the following months of enforced solitude, More wrote a longer defence of his conscience in *A Dialogue of Comfort Against Tribulation*. He gave great care to both the form and content of this work, now regarded as a classic of Christian prison and consolation literature. We know that More owned a copy of Boethius' famous prison work, *Of the Consolation of Philosophy*, written before his execution in about AD 524. For More *comfort* was a derivative of the Latin word *fortis* meaning strong. He understood it to be that which can give strength or courage to endure in a time of acute human suffering. Comfort or consolation literature was the medieval equivalent of modern counselling techniques used to deal with trauma and stress. In Christian spirituality and theology the Holy Spirit was understood as the true Comforter, the one who gave courage, strength and hope to the human heart.

More needed to comfort (strengthen) his family, and yet he had no easy solution nor the hope of quick release to offer them. He owed them an explanation for an apparent act of folly, which would profoundly affect their lives, and leave them financially destitute. He had to convince them that his death would not be a tragedy – as he was a public figure, his fall from power and probable execution had all the elements of a classic tragedy. He returned to the theme he had explored with Erasmus twenty-five years earlier: Christian wisdom which appears folly to the worldly-wise. *A Dialogue of Comfort* (1534) was More's version of his friend's *In Praise of Folly* (1511), but written in circumstances they could never have envisaged.

Because his writings could be confiscated at any time, and used against him, More had to conceal his real purpose under a semi-fictitious setting. He devised a story set in Hungary, then under siege by the Turks. The date he chose was 1527, just after the first invasion of Hungary by Suleiman the Magnificent, and just before the second devastating battle. These recent, terrifying events under a Turkish tyrant, and their indirect application to More's situation under Henry VIII, would be evident to his family. In the story an elderly uncle, Antony, and a young nephew, Vincent, try to face up to their situation. The old man is sick in bed, in a city (Buda) ringed by enemy troops. What comfort can one take facing a hopeless situation of prolonged siege, defeat, captivity, and almost certain death? What can one rely on when one's world is falling apart? *A Dialogue of Comfort* is a parable or story about how one terrified Christian (Vincent) is enabled to make a transition from paralysing fear, to one of total trust in God, whatever the future may hold.

As More saw it, his beloved 'common corps of Christendom' was threatened from the outside by the Turk, and from the inside by the heretic and the unjust tyrant. More wanted his personal battle for integrity to be seen as part of a wider battle between good and evil being fought in other parts of Christendom and the wider world. Tribulation or suffering is part of the human condition, whether it is experienced as international disaster, as family loss, or as inner anguish. So at the literal level (for the casual reader) More's story was about the recent, calamitous, Turkish invasion; at a deeper level he was writing to help his family and friends make sense of his choice and their fate; at the deepest level his own stronger self (Antony) dialogued with his weaker self (Vincent), or his Christian soul dialogued with God, by means of the comfort of Scripture, God's true word. More was also writing to comfort and strengthen himself against his coming ordeal.

Because of its multi-layered meanings *A Dialogue of Comfort* is not an easy book to read. The reader needs considerable help to understand its literary form: suffering or 'tribulation' considered from the perspectives of **Faith** (Book One), **Hope** (Book Two) and **Charity** (Book Three). More intended to show how it was possible for a Christian to move from a mood in which the mind is gripped by fear and despair, to one in which the *mind is* redeemed by faith, the *memory and imagination* by hope, and the *heart* by charity. At its core is a central fear or conflict: fear of persecution, physical torture and 'a cruel and shameful death'. The actual discussion of this central fear is suspended until book three, but it is before the 'eye of the imagination' throughout. The conflict is resolved only when the fearful human emotions are exorcized by love and the promise of eternal life, the only true comfort in adversity.

In **Book One** (On Faith), Antony and Vincent discuss the comfort which the collective wisdom of the human intellect can offer in time of suffering. The classical Stoic philosophers gave sound advice: on how to accept adversity with dignity, on being indifferent to the swings of fortune, or to wealth, reputation, even good health. But natural wisdom can only offer partial comfort; belief in God, and in God's word revealed in Scripture, is a further necessary step towards possessing sure comfort. However tiny the seed of faith is in our hearts, it can grow into a force that can move a mountain of tribulation. But it has to be an active, lively faith that *wants* God's comfort, a faith that does not get swallowed up by listless sorrow or raging anger.

So Antony outlines that kind of faith which builds upon, but goes beyond, rational human efforts to meet adversity. He gives some of the traditional theological arguments for accepting suffering as part of God's providence: suffering can be medicinal,

or educative, or corrective. God can use suffering to chasten sinners, to purify the good, to deepen the superficial. The problem of
undeserved suffering is faced. If we suffer this patiently, our
reward will be great. Vincent is impressed, but not entirely convinced. Is it possible to pray for suffering to be removed or avoided?
Yes, replies Antony, provided we leave the outcome to God,
because from the perspective of faith, some suffering may be a gift.

The great contribution of **Book Two** (On Hope), is More's recognition that the human mind, especially in time of anguish, will not
be satisfied by purely intellectual arguments. So in Book Two,
Antony tries a different strategy with his nephew, moving from
what may be *read in books*, to what may be *seen and heard* in the rich
complexity of human living. True comfort is related to hope, that
gift of the human imagination which can help to redeem the mind
from fear. Book Two stresses the importance of relaxation and
'proper pleasant talking', and is full of merry tales and jokes. But it
also explores black humour and the darker side of life without
hope. It is deliberately long and rambling, full of digressions which
may irk the contemporary reader. But it must have delighted
More's family, who knew well his method of rambling off at a tan-
gent, only eventually to target what he really wanted to say.

For More, Christian hope ultimately meant hope that there
would be life after death. And more immediately, it was grounded
in the conviction that God's enabling grace would support the
Christian in all circumstances of this present life, without exception. Evil, understood as the activity of a personalized devil or
demons, was part of More's mental world; the subversive activity of
the 'princes and potentates of these dark regions' put the human
soul in grave moral danger. The devil, rather than the Grand Turk,
the English king, or the heretic, was the real enemy. The Christian
life is a wrestling match or struggle between the forces of good and
evil: God alone is the ground of our hope that good will prevail.

The ability to hope and to endure was also related to sound
common sense and healthy human psychology. The mirth and

the many tales about human folly and absurdity were intended to relax both Vincent and the reader. Laughter is itself transformative and has its role to play in adjusting perspective, especially a tragic perspective. Antony admits that he is of 'nature even half a giglet [jokester] or more'. Merriment is good sauce for the meat, or a sweetener for the medicine, of theological discussion. So the very structure of their conversation sets out to be an act of hope in the middle of tribulation.

Antony and Vincent now concentrate on 'the anxiety which assaults the mind when a man is brought to trial', or to a time of acute testing. He addresses four kinds of temptation, suggested by Psalm 90:5–6: 'You will not fear the terror of the night, nor the arrow that flies by day, nor the pestilence that stalks in darkness, nor the destruction that wastes at noonday.' The element common to all four temptations is fear. The first temptation, the night fear, suggests the inner reality of a soul trapped in an anxiety state, with the possibility that it may ultimately be driven to self-destruction. Next comes the 'arrow by day' or pride in all its forms. Then the 'pestilence that stalks by darkness': the covetousness, lust and entanglement of worldly business. Finally the noonday devil, or open persecution and the threat of a violent and painful death. Armed with the shield of God's truth, the Christian can fight these four temptations.

Under the image of the 'terror of the night', Antony and Vincent explore the psychology of fear and anxiety in its many forms: presumption, scrupulousness, cowardice, despair and suicide. Reason is brought to bear on each problem by directly confronting it. The author gives more attention to suicide than to any other form of temptation in the entire work. Arguably it is the first significant treatment of the topic in the English language. Antony (More) has had considerable experience of would-be suicides: 'Many have I heard of and with some have I talked myself that have been sore encumbered with that temptation, and marked I not a little the manner of them'. Like most of his contemporaries, the author attributed the temptation to suicide to the suggestions of the devil. Yet his experience and intuitive insight were far greater than either the psychological and theological tools at his disposal for correct diagnosis.

To what extent was suicide More's own personal temptation, especially considering his fear of torture? He clearly tried to exorcize the fear by considering what drove people to it. He noted that war and invasion can pose exceptionally difficult moral choices, and that in extreme circumstances some felt justified in taking their own lives. Others chose suicide because they were subject to forms of religious self-deception or derangement: the widow who 'arranged' her martyrdom so that she might be canonized; the deluded monk who 'aspired' to martyrdom; the grisly example of a carver who asked his wife to crucify him so that he could literally follow Christ.

Evidence from the prison letters suggests that More was worried most by the possibility of self-delusion. The problem of the self-deluded person was indirectly related to the problem of martyrdom. Martyrdom, if self-chosen, or hastily entered into, or in any way directly sought, could be regarded as a form of self-destruction. Right discernment in the events which finally bring a person to a choice between life or death, has to be very careful. The act of human self-destruction is the triumph of death in every sense, and the antithesis of Christ's salvific act, which is a triumph of life. A Christian martyr has to make a very finely balanced choice. Was More's personal choice *really* necessary, or was he deluding himself that he had no other choice?

The arrow that flies by day, pride, and the pestilence in the darkness, acquisitiveness, are temptations of prosperity, so they provide a short dramatic interlude before the final terrible onslaught of the noonday devil: when the worst befalls.

Book Three (On Charity) moves beyond faith and hope, to the only sure comfort in extreme adversity: the love of God anchored in the human heart and made visible in the passion and death of

Jesus Christ. It begins as a calm and rational meditation on how to preserve moral courage in the face of death. Poverty, disgrace and death are not to be compared to a virtuous life; the short act of execution can be quicker and less painful than a long and lingering disease; physical imprisonment is only an intensified instance of life in a world which is quite like a prison anyway, and full of suffering. Such rational arguments were intended to prevent the tendency to over-dramatize the situation, or to fall into self-pity.

Gradually Antony and Vincent, who is by now much stronger, draw less comfort from rational arguments, and more from the biblical examples of those who kept faith in God, especially those unjustly imprisoned: Job, Joseph, Daniel, John the Baptist, Stephen, Peter, Paul. But above all there is the example of Jesus the prisoner:

> *Our saviour was himself taken prisoner for our sake, and prisoner was he carried, and prisoner was he kept ... unto the end of his passion. The time of his imprisonment, I grant well was not long, but as for hard handling which our hearts most abhor, he had as much in that short while as many men ... in much longer time.*
> (DC 286)

Book Three gradually becomes *an experience* of receiving strength and comfort through an extended meditation on the passion and death of Jesus the prisoner. He also felt fear and anguish, but overcame both. He is our pattern of moral integrity and of trust in God. His victory can strengthen and empower those facing acute suffering and a shameful death. The conversion of Vincent's mind by faith, his will and imagination by hope, and his heart by charity or the redeeming love of Christ, turns him into a conqueror (Latin *vincens*). When the discerning heart, conscience, is in the hands of God, love can conquer all, even sickening fear, and lack of courage.

> *Let us be of good comfort, for since we be by our faith very sure*
> *that holy Scripture is the word of God, and the word of God cannot*
> *be but true and we see that ... if God makes us and keep us good*
> *men, as he hath promised to do ... then saith holy Scripture: Unto*
> *good folk all things turn to good (Romans 8:28). God is faithful,*
> *which suffereth you not to be tempted above that you may bear but*
> *giveth also with the temptation a way out (1 Corinthians 10:13).*
> (DC 254–5)

Gethsemane: More and the Sadness of Christ

The real ending of *A Dialogue of Comfort Against Tribulation* lies
beyond his writing, in More's trial and execution. Until the very
point of martyrdom, he could not be certain that he would not
betray himself in some way. The fear of what was to come constituted his Gethsemane: his own agony in the garden. Not surpris-
ingly, More turned again to meditate on the passion of Christ. His
last work was *On the Sadness, Weariness, Fear and Prayer of Christ
before his Passion*, usually referred to as *The Sadness of Christ*. This
is really a commentary on the texts of the four gospel accounts of
Christ's agony in the garden, interspersed with personal prayer
and reflection. Either by design or accident, it stops at the point of
Jesus' arrest.

More wrote it very quickly, probably in about twenty-five sit-
tings, in May/June 1535. He wrote in Latin, and so for an educated audience, probably the same as that for which *Utopia* had been
intended. More focused not on the physical but on the mental
anguish and human feelings of Jesus during the time in the Garden of Gethsemane. More had always held that human beings
have the power to shape their own destiny, with the help of God's
grace. The freedom of following conscience was to him their
ultimate dignity. For a Christian giving witness by his own death,
this involved being refashioned in the likeness of the suffering
humanity of Jesus Christ.

Humanist theology more usually affirmed the dignity and greatness of human beings made in the image and likeness of God. In the agony in the garden it was the vulnerability and weakness of the humanity of Jesus Christ that were revealed. God can, and does, raise up 'brave champions' who publicly confess their faith and expose themselves to a martyr's death with great heroism. But God, in his mercy, has given Christians the example of Christ, who in his weakness and reluctance to face his death, sought his strength from God alone. More need not be ashamed to follow such a master.

More meditated on Jesus in the garden, praying in the darkness in agony; the apostles were sleeping, like many church leaders since; Judas was awake, doing the evil that would lead to his final despair. During those hours Jesus fought and won his battle. More focused his meditation on the moment when Jesus freely decided and knowingly accepted his destiny: passion and death. He imagined Jesus about to be taken captive, foreseeing the sufferings of future Christians, his comrades-in-arms, who will fight against the prince of darkness and all his human agents. The whole of history, not merely the hour of Christ's passion, is an 'hour of darkness'. This imagined speech of Christ is a triumphant, classical oration, covering eleven pages of the original manuscript. The moment of betrayal and arrest seems to be defeat, but in reality the time of the power of darkness is very short. Jesus confronts his enemies:

> But this hour and this power of darkness are not only given to you now against me, but such an hour and such a brief power of darkness will also be given to other governors and other Caesars against other disciples of mine. And this too will truly be the power of darkness. For whatever my disciples endure and whatever they say, they will not endure by their own strength or say of themselves, but conquering through my strength they will win their souls by patience ... (TW 284)

Judas betrayed his master by an acted lie, which was the opposite of what it was meant to signify: an act of friendship. Jesus dealt with what he knew to be treachery, with patience and gentleness. After Jesus' arrest 'all his disciples abandoned him and fled'.

On 12 June 1535, the Lieutenant of the Tower and others came into More's cell and ordered the confiscation of his writing materials and books. Judas also entered his cell in the person of Sir Richard Rich; it was his version of the subsequent conversation between himself and More that was the cause of More's final conviction. Between 12 June and his trial on 1 July, More closed the shutters of his window and announced that his shop was closed.

$$(7)$$

The Morean Synthesis

No part of his life is more frequently or more gladly spoken of than his cheerful death. (MORE IN *UTOPIA*, ON THE DEATH OF A GOOD MAN)

Trial and Execution

On 28 June 1535 Thomas More was formally indicted for trea son, and on 1 July appeared on trial in Westminster Hall, the place where he had sat so often in judgement as Lord Chancellor. Treason trials were unfair and their conclusions predictable. More was not given a copy of the grounds for indictment before his trial, and only had it read out to him in court. He had to conduct his own defence, could call on no witnesses, and could expect the jury to comply with the wishes of the bench. More did not complain of his unjust hearing; this was usual practice in treason trials. His intention was to defend himself as well as he possibly could, with all his skill and ability as a lawyer. Because of his ill health and infirmity More was allowed to remain seated while conducting his defence.

That defence was that he had never disclosed to anyone the reason for his refusal of the oath attached to the Act of Succession. In common law and in natural justice a man could not be tried for his thoughts. Silence was normally interpreted as consent rather than disapproval. Nevertheless, by his silence More was accused of 'falsely, traitorously and maliciously' depriving the King of his title of Supreme Head of the Church, 'to the contempt of the King and against his peace'. More replied:

> *Ye must understand that in things touching conscience, every true and good subject is more bound to have respect to his said conscience and to his soul than to any other thing in all the world ... when his conscience is in such sort as mine is, that is to say when the person giveth no occasion of slander, of tumult and sedition against his prince, as it is with me; for I assure you that I have not hitherto to this hour disclosed and opened my conscience and mind to any living person in all the world.* (N. HARPSFIELD, *THE LIFE AND DEATH OF SIR THOMAS MORE* 186)

It has been rightly said that 'More is that rare figure ... an establishment martyr' (Kenny). He feared sedition, or any act that would destabilize lawful government. Throughout his trial he always spoke of the King with love, respect and loyalty. He did not seek to influence others, so what he *thought* in his innermost mind was known only to God. As he had previously said to Cromwell:

> *I am the King's true and faithful subject ... and pray for his highness and all the realm. I do nobody no harm, I say none harm, I think none harm ... but wish everybody good. And if this be not enough to keep a man alive, in good faith I long not to live.* (SL 63)

More was condemned because of the evidence of Richard Rich, who swore that in a conversation with More in prison, the latter had broken his silence and declared that Parliament could not make Henry VIII Supreme Head of the Church in England. More insisted that they had spoken of hypothetical cases, not of the matter before the judges. Rich's word was believed, without a corroborating witness. Only after More had been condemned did he finally break his silence and reveal the reasons for his stand in conscience. He had been charged on an indictment insufficient to condemn any man, under the terms of an Act of Parliament which was itself unlawful, since it failed to uphold the liberties of the Church as stated in Magna Carta (1215). Finally, he argued that the universal law of Christendom had a prior claim on his obedience above that of the law of a single realm. According to one biographer, More gave one hint as to the real reasons for his trial: 'I call and appeal to God whose only sight pierceth onto the depths of man's heart to be my witness ... it is not for the supremacy that you seek my blood, as for that I would not condescend to the marriage' (HARPSFIELD 186).

More was condemned to death, and his sentence was 'mercifully' commuted to beheading. It was carried out on 6 July 1535, on Tower Green. His final prison letters to his family and friends were free of rancour, bitterness or self-regard, and were full of concern for those who had suffered so much because of his decision. He had recovered his peace of mind and sense of humour, so often absent in his controversial writings. His last prison prayers and the annotations on the side of his well-used psalter, testify to the depths of his faith and to his trust in God's grace that he would be faithful to the end. He died, as he had lived, 'the King's loyal servant, but God's first'.

More's Life and Thought: An Assessment

More's trial proceedings, and his subsequent execution, are so well known and recorded that they must constitute a final statement about what he thought, in relation to conscience and the human person. More's famous refusal to allow the state to dictate what he thought or believed in his innermost mind, because a *cause célèbre* in Europe within weeks of his execution. A Paris newsletter was in circulation by mid-July 1535, and his biographers, Roper and Harpsfield, had access to eye-witness accounts and to family memories. The political and constitutional implications of More's final act have passed into the English parliamentary heritage.

More's discreet and political silence has made the precise cause of his death a little difficult to pinpoint. Henry VIII and his secretary Cromwell regarded the sovereign action of the king in Parliament, embodied in statute, as the highest expression of binding law. They were, in modern parlance, 'little Englanders'. More took the older view that English law should be tested against the law of nature, and against the consensus of Christendom embodied in the decrees of General Councils. England was not just an island 'sovereign unto itself'; it had its rightful independence but had also to consider its relationship and responsibilities to the wider community of which it was a part. More believed in the unity of Christendom, symbolized by the leadership of the pope. He died because he refused to play his part in any process which might dismantle or harm that unity. This seemed to many of his political colleagues to be traditionalist, bigoted and against the nation's best interests.

It does not detract from the integrity of More's stand to say that it is now generally recognized – with hindsight – that the breakup of European Christendom, and the emergence of the nation state, was part of an inevitable shift from late-medieval to modern European society. Christendom broke up for political, economic and social reasons as much as for religious ones. In each country, and in many cities throughout Europe, the self-interest of prince or city council played its part in the reception or non-reception of religious reformation. England was no exception. Ironically More had most in common with those whom he implacably opposed: religious leaders like Luther and Tyndale, who were motivated by a genuine desire to preach the gospel.

More's religious vision of a united Christendom was inseparable from his political vision of a Europe united by a shared heritage and a common culture. He constantly expressed his hatred for war, which disrupted the internal and external peace of European nations. While Christendom in its late-medieval shape can never be revived, the idea that the nation state belongs to a greater

whole – either the European or the world community – is a vision
many can share today. Thomas More was not only a great Eng-
lishman but also a great European; he perceived that England's
national interests were served by belonging to, rather than being
in isolation from, the rest of the continent. His Utopian vision
embraced the whole world.

More made no claims to be a professional theologian or philosopher, and positively disliked abstract thought. He claimed to be a
Christian humanist interested in every aspect of human life as it
related to the Christian vocation. More's thought was always
directed to practical action; for him a Christian was called to serve
God 'especially in the mind' as directed outwards towards the
complexities of life. In the journey through life there are no blue-
prints, no exact precedents telling men and women how to act in
any situation; there are only general principles which have to be
applied to particular situations. A good Christian had to work out,
with the aid of reason, the help of God's grace, and the collective
wisdom of the Christian community, how to discern right action.
Conscience as right discernment applied to all More's life, not only
to his decisions as a judge, or to his final choice.

As this study has shown, More's thought and action fall into
three distinct phases: early humanist, public life, and the prison
experience. As a young humanist More relished belonging to a circle of friends with whom he shaped his political, educational and
literary ideals. His early writings include pithy epigrams, English
poetry, four long letter-essays in defence of humanism, and a History of Richard III. Utopia was to be the greatest and most enduring
expression of his political ideals, and is a work which continues to
challenge and to invite criticism of social injustice, which is the
consequence of human greed and self-interest.

In More's second period, that of his public life, he provided an
enduring example of honesty and integrity in the exercise of his
duties. More's time as Chancellor was marked by concern for the
poor and for the reform of common law; but it was also marked by

harshness and intolerance towards heretics, to whom he denied the freedom of conscience he was soon to claim for himself. The limitations of a good man under pressure, as his world falls apart, are evident in More's controversial writings, of which the best must be his *Dialogue Concerning Heresies*. These polemical writings are difficult for a modern reader, and are the least relevant for contemporary life.

More's Tower experience yielded the devotional writings and letters of a great Christian who was prepared to suffer the loss of everything – position, wealth but most of all his beloved family – rather than compromise his conscience. He defended his choice with dignity, courage and lack of bitterness. Failed politicians usually are not noted for 'letting go' of public life and the part they may have played in it. More had played his part and now wanted to 'set the world at nought' and prepare himself to face God, his final judge. The depths of More's faith and spirituality were the fruit of a lifetime habit of prayer and of referring all things to God. He was discreet and humble about his spiritual life, though there are hints in his prison writings of the times he experienced joy and consolation during his lonely vigils. He had asked, 'The things good Lord that I pray for, give me thy grace to labour for'. The good works of human living had to be laboured for, but God was always at hand.

More's final gift to his family and friends was his conviction that this was not the end. 'Fare well, my dear child, and pray for me, and I shall for you and all your friends that we may meet merrily in heaven.' (SL 66) The best things in life: love, friendship, homely conversation, shared insight, festive meals, would be part of life with God in heaven, where we 'shall need no letters, where no wall shall separate us, and where no porter shall keep us from talking together' (SL 65).

Suggested Further Reading

More's Writings

The Yale Edition of *The Complete Works of St Thomas More*, 1963–1996, 15 volumes.

The Yale Edition of *Selected Works of St Thomas More* (with modernized spelling) Where possible these have been used in the present study.

St Thomas More: Selected Letters ed. E. F. Rogers 1961.

Utopia ed. E. Surtz (see below for alternative text), 1964.

The History of King Richard III, and

Selections from the English and Latin Poems ed. R. S. Sylvester, 1976.

A Dialogue of Comfort Against Tribulation ed. F. Manley, 1977.

The Tower Works: Devotional Writings ed. G. E. Haupt, 1980.

Thomas More's Prayer Book, 1969.

The Correspondence of Sir Thomas More ed. E. F. Rogers, Princeton, 1947.

Alternative edition of *Utopia* ed. G. M. Logan & R. M. Adams, Cambridge Texts in the History of Political Thought, 1989. Cited in text.

Biographies

Roper, William, *Life of Sir Thomas More* in the Everyman Edition, ed. E. E. Reynolds, or in *Two Early Tudor Lives* ed. R. S. Sylvester & D. P. Harding, Yale University Press, 1962. Cited in text.

Harpsfield, Nicholas, *The Life and Death of Sir Thomas More* (1557), Everyman edition with Roper's life, as above.

Stapleton, Thomas, *Life of Sir Thomas More* (1588), Burns & Oates, 1928.

Chambers, R. S., *Thomas More*, Jonathan Cape, 1935, Penguin, 1963.

Reynolds, E. E., *The Life and Death of St Thomas More: The Field is Won*, Burns & Oates, 1963.

Kenny, A., *Thomas More*, Oxford University Press, 1983.

Marius, R., *Thomas More*, J. M. Dent, 1985. Fullest revisionist study.

Martz, L. L., *Thomas More: The Search for the Inner Man*, Yale University Press, 1990. Four reprinted articles.

Humanism/Utopia

Bradshaw, B., and Duffy, E., eds. *Humanism, Reform and Reformation: The Career of Bishop John Fisher*, Cambridge University Press, 1989.

Fleisher, M., *Radical Reform and Political Persuasion in the Life and Writings of Thomas More*, Geneva, Libraire Droz, 1973.

Hexter, J. H., *The Biography of an Idea*, Princeton, 1952.

McConica, J., *Erasmus*, Oxford University Press, 1991.

McCutcheon, E. and Miller, C. H., *Utopia Revisited*, Moreana 118–19, Angers, 1994.

Olin, J. C., ed. *Interpreting Thomas More's Utopia*, Fordham, 1989.

Skinner, Q., 'Sir Thomas More's *Utopia* and the Language of Renaissance Humanism' in *Languages of Political Theory in Early Modern Europe*, Cambridge, 1987.

Baker-Smith, D., *More's Utopia*, HarperCollins Academic, 1991.

Public Life/Reign of Henry VIII

Duffy, E., *The Stripping of the Altars: Traditional Religion in England 1400–1580*, Yale University Press, 1992.

Guy, J. M., *The Public Career of Sir Thomas More*, Harvester Press 1980.

Gwyn, P., *The King's Cardinal: The Rise and Fall of Cardinal Wolsey*, 1990.

Rex, R., *Henry VIII and the English Reformation*, Macmillan, 1993.

Later Writings

Fox, A., *Thomas More: History and Providence*, Oxford, 1982. Particular attention to More as writer.

Gogan, B., *The Common Corps of Christendom: Ecclesiological Themes in the Writings of Sir Thomas More*, Brill, Leiden, 1982.

Luther, M., *Luther's Works*, eds. J. Pelican et al., St Louis & Philadelphia, 1955–.

Reynolds, E. E., *The Trial of St Thomas More*, London, Burns & Oates, 1964.

Articles and Collections

Introduction to each volume of the Yale Editions of the *Complete Works*. This study is especially indebted to

Martz, L. L. and Manley, F., introduction to CW12, *A Dialogue of Comfort Against Tribulation*, xix–clxvii.

Sylvester, R. S. & Marc'hadour, G., eds. *Essential Articles for the Study of Thomas More*, Connecticut, 1977.

Bradshaw, B., 'The Controversial Sir Thomas More', *Journal of Ecclesiastical History* 36:4, 535–569, 1985.

Index

Index